SCANDINAVIAN
Christmas

'Playing in the snow, enjoying warm drinks, baking, and being with people you love: that is Christmas.'

SCANDINAVIAN
Christmas

Trine Hahnemann

PHOTOGRAPHY BY LARS RANEK

Quadrille
PUBLISHING

Introduction

Christmas is my favourite time of year. I thrive in the winter months. I love the cold, the blue winter sky and, especially, the magical atmosphere when the world goes quiet, covered in snow.

I go a little crazy at Christmas; without a doubt my family would agree about that. The celebrations start on 1 December when I get out my Christmas decorations. I become pathetically happy when I unwrap all the little glass balls, my antique 'nisser' (elves), the ribbons, candles, stars, and – most of all – my little porcelain snowman. It is hard to explain the sheer happiness I feel when I am reunited with these small, ridiculous and to some extent useless items. After I have decorated the whole house I feel, for a short while, that everything is perfect.

I put in a lot of work to make Christmas great, I admit that, and I often take my vacation in December so I have time to do it all and enjoy it, too. But please don't feel under any pressure to do the same. It's completely missing the point of Christmas to be totally stressed out! Select just those things from this book that you would like to cook, and have fun. Christmas is about celebrating life and 'hygge', a Danish term that is almost untranslateable, but encompasses comfort, camaraderie, and good food and drink. So create your own celebrations on your own terms.

In this book I have opened up a window into my Christmas. It is fairly traditional, though with some new twists and turns, but also very emotional, because the season tends to heighten and amplify life itself. I hope you will enjoy my recipes and ideas, and remember that a lot of them can be useful all through the winter months.

Velbekommen!

Trine Hahnemann

CHRISTMAS BAKING

Christmas in Scandinavia is all about baking. My recipes are a mixture of family treasures and my own creations, but they are all founded in Scandinavian Christmas tradition, with little adjustments that I've made here and there.

I learned how to do the Christmas baking when I was very young... I think I was trying to create a sense of the festive traditions in a childhood dominated by left-wing activism, where Christmas was taboo! However, my grandparents celebrated Christmas in a wonderful way; my grandmother baked everything and I learned from her. (Later, my mother did a complete turn back to celebrating Christmas.)

The reason why you have to bake so many different things is that you need enough to last for the whole of December. You can't run out of cakes or, especially, cookies... and you should have at least three or four kinds ready, stored in your kitchen, for family, friends and unexpected visitors.
The recipes here are for special occasions, for Advent Sunday parties, for presents, or just for nibbling when you get in from work on a cold evening. Have fun with the baking, it doesn't have to be stressful and the finished product doesn't need to look perfect. Just get people together and have fun!

❄ LUCIA BREAD ❄ PULLA BREAD ❄ SPICED CHRISTMAS CAKE ❄ HONEY LAYER CAKE WITH ORANGE MOUSSE
❄ REDCURRANT-ALMOND CUPCAKES ❄ VANILLA COOKIES ❄ HONEY HEARTS
❄ ICED ALMOND HEARTS ❄ CRISP CINNAMON COOKIES ❄ PEPPER NUTS ❄ OAT COOKIES
❄ KLEJNER ❄ BROWN COOKIES ❄ HALLON COOKIES

'Christmas is my favourite time of year. I am a winter person, I love the cold and the way the world turns silent when covered in snow.'

'This season is all about being inside with candles and great comfort food.'

Lucia bread *Makes about 22*

Legend has it that, on 13 December 1764, a gentleman in Sweden was woken in the middle of the night by a beautiful voice. He saw a young woman in white, singing and dancing through his room. She had wings and was carrying a candle. It was Saint Lucia. She brought light, food and wine for comfort on what was, in the Gregorian calendar, the longest night of the year. We celebrate this fabled event every 13 December. Girls dress up in long white dresses and walk carrying lit candles, singing the beautiful Lucia carol. It's one of the favourite Christmas traditions and makes everyone well up! Somehow it makes you grateful for life.

YOU WILL NEED
40g fresh yeast (or 15g dried yeast if you really have to! We don't use dried yeast in Scandinavia)
500ml lukewarm whole milk
½ tsp saffron
200g salted butter, melted
1kg plain flour, plus more to dust
1 tsp salt
100g caster sugar
75g raisins, plus more to decorate
1 egg, beaten

Dissolve the yeast in the warm milk in a mixing bowl, then add the saffron and stir until the mixture turns yellow. Add the melted butter. In a separate mixing bowl, sift together the flour and salt, then stir in the sugar and raisins.

Pour the yeast mixture into the dry ingredients and stir until the dough comes cleanly from the edge of the bowl. Knead the dough on a floured work surface for 10 minutes, until it is shiny but not sticky. Return it to the bowl, cover with a clean tea towel and leave to rise for 1½ hours at room temperature.

Lightly knead the dough again on a floured work surface. Divide it into about 22 equal pieces. Roll them into sausages, then form them into different shapes, as seen in the photograph, curling up the ends. Stud each with a few raisins.

Place the breads on baking trays lined with baking parchment, cover with clean tea towels and leave to rise again for 30 minutes.

Preheat the oven to 180°C/350°F/gas mark 4. Brush the risen breads with the beaten egg and bake for 20–25 minutes, or until golden brown all over, then leave to cool on a wire rack.

Eat them as they are, or spread with chilled butter.

'Lucia breads often take the form of old Nordic mythological symbols, such as buckthorn and cats.'

Pulla bread *Makes 2 loaves*

In Scandinavia, December is the time for white, glossy, heavy bread, unlike the rye bread we favour for the rest of the year... Christmas is not the time for health food! This lovely loaf is best eaten the day it is baked, though after that it makes great toast.

YOU WILL NEED
50g fresh yeast (or 19g dried yeast
   if you really have to!)
250ml lukewarm whole milk
100g salted butter, softened,
   cut into small pieces
2 eggs, lightly beaten,
   plus 1 more to brush
700g plain flour, sifted,
   plus more to dust
100g golden caster sugar
½ tsp salt
1 tbsp cardamom seeds, crushed
   in a mortar and pestle
100g raisins
50g blanched almonds, chopped,
   plus more to sprinkle

Dissolve the yeast in the warm milk in a large mixing bowl, then add the butter and eggs. In a separate bowl, mix the flour, sugar, salt and cardamom. Mix this into the yeast mixture with the raisins and almonds. Now knead the dough on a floured surface for five minutes.

Cover the bowl with a clean tea towel and leave to rise in a warm place for one hour, or until the dough has doubled in size.

Now punch down the dough ('knock it back'), and let it rise again for 30 minutes. Divide the dough in two. Roll each piece into a rectangular shape, then cut each rectangle into three long 'fingers'. Plait three strands of dough together to form a braid, pressing in the ends, then repeat with the other three strands. Place both loaves on a baking tray lined with baking parchment, cover once more with clean tea towels and leave to rise for 30 minutes.

Preheat the oven to 200°C/400°F/gas mark 6. Brush the loaves with beaten egg, sprinkle with a few more almonds, then bake in the hot oven for 25–30 minutes, or until golden. Leave to rest on a wire rack for at least 10 minutes, then serve plain, or spread with butter and jam.

Spiced Christmas cake *Serves 12*

This is a typical afternoon tea cake eaten all through the winter months, here decorated for the festivities with white chocolate hearts. Using spices in baking is a Scandinavian tradition dating back to the Middle Ages.

YOU WILL NEED

225g salted butter, plus more
   for the tin
4 large eggs
225g dark muscovado sugar
330g plain flour
2 tsp baking powder
1 tsp ground cinnamon
1 tsp ground ginger
100ml whole milk
finely grated zest of 1 organic orange
200g good-quality white chocolate,
   plus more to adhere (optional)
icing sugar, to serve (optional)

Preheat the oven to 175°C/350°F/gas mark 4, and butter a 22cm round cake tin (or use a heart-shaped tin, 22cm at its widest point, if you prefer). Melt the remaining butter and cool it down.

Whisk the eggs and sugar in a big bowl until the mixture holds a ribbon trail for eight to 10 seconds after the whisk has been lifted. In a separate bowl, sift together the flour, baking powder, cinnamon and ginger.

Stir the flour mixture and milk, alternately and only a little at a time, into the egg mixture, until just combined. Add the orange zest. Fold together as lightly as possible. Finally, stir the melted butter into the mixture.

Pour the batter into the prepared tin and bake for 50–55 minutes. Leave to cool on a wire rack.

Melt the white chocolate and place in a small piping bag, snip off the end and pipe hearts on a piece of baking parchment. Leave to set, then peel them off the parchment and arrange on the cake, sticking them on with a little more melted white chocolate, if you want. Sprinkle with icing sugar, if you like, and serve.

'I have a special place in my heart for plain cakes with spices.'

Honey layer cake with orange mousse

Serves 12

This is for a special occasion; we always serve layer cakes for a celebration or a birthday. In more rural areas, layer cakes are more common; in fact, in many regions you are more likely to be invited to a 'cake table' than to dinner. At these gatherings, you start with a wheat bun, then take a piece of both coffee cake and layer cake, nibbling on cookies in between. Scandinavia is cake paradise.

YOU WILL NEED

For the cake
salted butter, for the tin
3 eggs, separated,
  plus 1 whole egg
100g caster sugar
225g honey
250g plain flour
2 tsp baking powder
½ tsp ground cloves
½ tsp ground ginger

For the orange mousse
6 gelatine sheets
50g icing sugar
200ml freshly squeezed orange juice
1 tbsp finely grated unwaxed
  lemon zest
3 tbsp finely grated organic
  orange zest
500ml double cream, lightly whipped

To serve
5 oranges
3–4 tbsp Grand Marnier,
  or orange juice
finely grated zest of 1 organic orange

For the cake, preheat the oven to 150°C/300°F/gas mark 2. Butter the sides of a 24cm round springform cake tin and line the base with baking parchment.

Beat the egg yolks, whole egg, sugar and honey until the mixture holds a ribbon trail for eight to 10 seconds after the whisk has been lifted. In a separate bowl, sift together the flour, baking powder and spices, then fold this into the batter. Whisk the egg whites until stiff and gently fold them into the batter, too. Pour the batter into the prepared tin and bake in the oven for about 45 minutes. Make sure the cake is done by sticking a knitting needle into it. If nothing sticks to the needle, it is ready. Remove the cake from the tin and leave to cool on a wire rack.

For the mousse, soak the gelatine in cold water for five to 10 minutes. Sift the icing sugar into a separate bowl and mix in the orange juice and lemon and orange zests.

Remove the gelatine from the water, squeezing out the excess, and place in a small bowl over a pan of simmering water (make sure the bowl does not touch the water). Heat until melted, shaking the gelatine gently without stirring. Stir the melted gelatine into the orange mixture, then pour the liquid through a sieve. Fold it little by little into the whipped cream, then place in the fridge for about one hour.

To serve, cut the oranges into segments. Cut the cake into three horizontal layers and sprinkle the bottom and middle layers with the Grand Marnier or orange juice. Place the bottom layer of cake on a serving dish. Spread with one-third of the mousse, then arrange over a layer of orange segments. Repeat with the next layer, then place the last layer of cake on top. Spread with the remaining mousse and orange segments and sprinkle with the orange zest. Let the cake rest for 30 minutes, then serve.

'Every year I bake two batches of Vaniljekranse. They are my husband's favourite, and he always empties the cookie jar.'

Redcurrant-almond cupcakes *Makes 18*

Tasty and easy to make, these are fun to decorate, especially if you involve children (though, often, they are more interested in decorating than eating them!). I like the tart redcurrants here.

Preheat the oven to 200°C/400°F/gas mark 6. Beat the butter and sugar until fluffy. Add the eggs one at a time, beating after each addition. Mix the flour, baking powder and almonds in a separate bowl, then mix into the batter with the milk. Add the redcurrants. Line the holes of a cupcake tin with paper cases and fill each two-thirds full (you may have to bake in batches). Bake for 30 minutes, then cool on a wire rack.

Mix the egg whites and icing sugar, divide between small bowls and add a different food colour to each, then use to ice the cakes.

YOU WILL NEED
For the cupcakes
250g salted butter
225g caster sugar
3 eggs
350g plain flour, sifted
2 tsp baking powder
150g ground almonds
250ml whole milk
150g frozen redcurrants
   (or other berries)

For the icing
1–2 egg whites
150g icing sugar
selection of food colours

Vanilla cookies *Makes about 80*

'Vaniljekranse' are the most popular Danish cookie and we form them with a special press, though it's easy to make them without. Use vanilla pods for the best flavour and the tiny black seeds.

Split the vanilla pods lengthways and scrape out the seeds with a knife. Mix the sugar and flour in a bowl, then rub in the butter with your fingertips. Add the egg and vanilla seeds, working with your fingers until the dough forms a ball. Knead on a lightly floured surface for one or two minutes, wrap in cling film and chill overnight.

When ready to bake, preheat the oven to 200°C/400°F/gas mark 6. Roll the dough into sausages 1 x 5–6cm long. Curl each into a ring and press the ends together. Place the cookies on a baking tray lined with baking parchment and bake for about seven minutes. (You will need to bake in batches.) Cool on a wire rack and store in an airtight tin for three to four weeks.

YOU WILL NEED
2 vanilla pods
250g caster sugar
500g plain flour, sifted,
   plus more to dust
375g cold salted butter,
   cut into small pieces
1 egg, beaten

Honey hearts *Makes 7 large, 15 middle-sized and 13 small*

Spiced honey cakes are a famous speciality from Christiansfelt, dating back to 1780, and it simply would not be Christmas without these… I eat them guiltily all through December for afternoon tea. They are one of the first things I bake in late November. It's very important to remember that the full flavour of the honey in these only really comes out after a week, so bake them well in advance of Christmas. They become softer as they mature. They can be used as Christmas tree decorations (iced with white icing, not chocolate). They are often heart-shaped, but can also be formed into men, women or Santa. If you can find baker's ammonia and baker's potash, use 1 tsp and 2 tsp respectively, and omit the baking powder and bicarbonate of soda, to keep the cookies soft for longer.

YOU WILL NEED
500g good-quality honey
3 egg yolks
200ml buttermilk
500g plain flour, plus more to dust
100g rye flour
2 tsp baking powder
½ tsp bicarbonate of soda
2 tsp ground cinnamon
1 tsp ground cloves
1 tsp ground allspice

For the tempered chocolate
400–500g dark chocolate
    (50–60 per cent cocoa solids),
    finely chopped

Melt the honey and leave it to cool. Add the egg yolks and buttermilk and mix well. In a separate bowl, sift together the flours, baking powder, bicarbonate of soda and spices, then fold them into the honey mixture.

On a floured work surface, knead the dough until smooth. Wrap it in cling film and chill for at least 24 hours.

When ready to bake, preheat the oven to 170°C/340°F/gas mark 3½. Sprinkle the dough with a little flour and place it between two sheets of baking parchment. Roll the dough between the parchments to 1cm thick. Peel off the top layer of parchment and cut out hearts with different sized cutters, until all the dough has been used.

Place the cookies on a baking tray lined with baking parchment. Bake for 12 minutes, then cool on a wire rack. (You may need to bake in batches.) Store in an airtight tin for about a week before covering them with tempered chocolate (see below).

Cover the hearts in the chocolate and place on a tray lined with baking parchment. Let cool until set, then store in an airtight tin. We usually decorate each with a small glossy picture. They keep for two to three weeks.

TEMPERED CHOCOLATE You will need a sugar thermometer. Melt two-thirds of the chocolate in a bowl over a pan of simmering water (the bowl must not touch the water). When it has reached 50°C (120°F), add the rest of the chocolate. Mix well until melted. Gently heat until it reaches 31°C (90°F). Now it is ready to use.

Iced almond hearts *Makes 40*

These taste lovely, but I always use half of them for decoration, hanging them up in a window or on the Christmas tree.

Mix the sugar, flour and almonds in a bowl. Rub in the butter with your fingertips until coarse crumbs are formed. Work in the egg with your fingers until you get an even dough. Wrap in cling film and leave to rest in the fridge for one hour.

When ready to bake, preheat the oven to 200°C/400°F/gas mark 6. Roll out the dough on a lightly floured surface and cut out hearts. Make a hole in each, to hang them up. Place them on a baking tray lined with baking parchment. (You may need to bake in batches.) Bake for five minutes, then cool on a wire rack. Mix the egg whites and icing sugar, add the food colour and decorate the cookies. Hang up, or store in an airtight tin for up to three weeks.

YOU WILL NEED
For the cookies
200g caster sugar
200g plain flour, sifted, plus more to dust
75g blanched almonds, finely ground
200g cold salted butter, cut into small pieces
1 egg, beaten

For the icing
1–2 egg whites
150g icing sugar
red food colour

Crisp cinnamon cookies
Makes about 65

My favourite cookie. I remember stealing them from the jar as a child, performing dangerous acrobatic feats to reach them! If you can get baker's ammonia, use it instead of baking powder.

Sift the flour and baking powder into a bowl and add the zest and sugar. Rub in the butter until coarse crumbs form. Work in the egg, then knead on a lightly floured surface for two minutes, wrap in cling film and chill for one hour, or overnight.

Preheat the oven to 200°C/400°F/gas mark 6. Sprinkle the dough with flour, place between sheets of baking parchment and roll out thinly. Peel off the parchment and cut out shapes (keep them to 5–6cm). Place on a lined baking tray. (You will need to bake in batches.) In a bowl, mix the cinnamon and demerara. Brush each cookie with egg, then sprinkle with the cinnamon mix. Bake for nine to 10 minutes, until golden, then cool on a wire rack. Store in an airtight tin; they keep for up to four weeks.

YOU WILL NEED
For the cookies
375g plain flour, plus more to dust
1 tsp baking powder
1 tsp finely grated unwaxed lemon zest
125g light soft brown sugar
250g cold salted butter, cut into small pieces
1 large egg, beaten

For the topping
2 tsp ground cinnamon
50g demerara sugar
1 egg, beaten

'Have fun baking your cookies. They don't have to be perfect.'

Pepper nuts *Makes 120*

Fun to make and easy for children to help with. These are part of everyday life in December, and are served everywhere. Don't leave the jar overnight where there is a light on, or the 'nisser' (elves) will come and steal them! The name of these comes from the spices used; there is no pepper in them.

Sift together the flour, baking powder and spices. Melt the butter and stir it into the flour mixture. Add the sugar and egg and knead the dough on a floured work surface until smooth. Leave to rest for one hour at room temperature.

Preheat the oven to 180°C/350°F/gas mark 4. Form the dough into thin sausages. Cut into small pieces, then roll each into a ball. Place them, each a little apart from the next, on a baking tray lined with baking parchment. (You will need to bake in batches.) Bake for 10 minutes, then cool on a wire rack. Store in an airtight tin for up to four weeks.

YOU WILL NEED
375g plain flour, plus more to dust
½ tsp baking powder
½ tsp freshly grated nutmeg
½ tsp ground ginger
2 tsp ground cinnamon
175g salted butter
180g dark brown soft sugar
1 egg, beaten

Oat cookies *Makes about 35*

My newest cookie recipe and so easy to make. My son really loves these, so they will be part of my Christmas tradition from now on! Rye or spelt flakes work really well in place of the oats.

Preheat the oven to 180°C/350°F/gas mark 4. Melt the butter and mix it with the rolled oats or rye or spelt flakes in a bowl. Add the sugar and eggs. In another bowl, mix the flour, baking powder, orange zest and salt. Stir this into the oat mixture.

Use two teaspoons to drop small mounds of the mixture on to a baking tray lined with baking parchment, spacing them out well. (You may need to bake in batches.)

Bake in the oven for about 10 minutes, then leave to cool a little before transferring to a wire rack. Cool and store in an airtight tin for up to three weeks.

YOU WILL NEED
150g salted butter
125g jumbo rolled oats
   or rye or spelt flakes
250g caster sugar
2 eggs, beaten
2 tbsp plain flour, sifted
2 tsp baking powder
2 tsp finely grated organic
   orange zest
pinch of salt

'One type of these cookies is crunchy and hard, the other soft and more like a doughnut in texture.'

Klejner I *Makes 30*

These are lovely if well executed, so an oil thermometer is vital. They are small and delightfully crunchy.

Mix the flour, sugar, cardamom and lemon zest in a mixing bowl, then rub in the butter with your fingertips. Stir in the eggs and cream to get a firm dough, then knead well on a lightly floured surface. Wrap in cling film and chill for one hour.

Roll out the dough on a floured surface to 5mm thick. With a sharp knife – or a fluted ravioli wheel – cut it into 2½ x 8cm strips. Make a slit in the centre of each. Pull one end through each slit, twisting the dough.

Heat the oil to 160°C (320°F), using a thermometer to check the temperature. If the oil is too hot the klejner will burn and, if it is too cool, they won't be crisp. Fry two or three at a time, turning once, until golden on both sides, then drain on kitchen paper. When cold, serve, or save in an airtight container for up to three weeks.

YOU WILL NEED
500g plain flour, sifted, plus more to dust
175g caster sugar
1 tsp ground cardamom seeds
finely grated zest of 1 unwaxed lemon
125g salted butter, cut into small pieces
3 eggs, beaten
4 tbsp double cream
vegetable oil or shortening, to deep-fry

Klejner II *Makes 18*

The Norwegian version, big, soft and lovely with icing. Eat them on the day you make them, and serve with Gløgg (see page 61).

Dissolve the yeast in the milk. Melt the butter and let it cool down a little, then mix it into the eggs. Split the vanilla pod lengthways and scrape the seeds into the milk with a knife, then pour in the butter mixture. Put the flour in a large bowl with the sugar and cardamom. Now mix the flour into the milk mixture, first with a wooden spoon, then kneading. Return it to the bowl, cover with a tea towel and leave to rise for one hour. Roll out on a floured surface to 1cm thick, then cut into 2½ x 8cm strips as above (these will double in size when cooked). Make a slit in the centre of each.

Heat the vegetable oil to 160°C (320°F), using a thermometer. Fry and drain as above, then cool. Mix the icing sugar and lemon juice and place in a piping bag. Ice the klejner as you like, then leave to set for 10 minutes. Serve, or store as above.

YOU WILL NEED
50g fresh yeast (or 19g dried yeast if you really have to!)
150ml lukewarm whole milk
100g salted butter
2 eggs, beaten
1 vanilla pod
500g plain flour, sifted, plus more to dust
50g caster sugar
1 tsp ground cardamom
vegetable oil or shortening, to deep-fry
150g icing sugar
juice from 1 lemon

Brown cookies *Makes about 175*

My mother makes me a batch of this 'Brunkager' dough every December, then I bake them: a treasured gift! If you can find baker's ammonia, add 1½ tsp; it makes these even crisper. Use 100g candied mixed peel, if that's all you can buy.

Melt the butter, syrup and muscovado in a saucepan, stirring until smooth. Cool a little, then add the almonds, candied zests and spices. Leave until cold. Mix in the flour and knead until smooth. Form into two or three 4–5cm-thick logs and wrap in cling film. To bring out the full flavour, chill for at least two days and up to a month.

When ready to bake, preheat the oven to 175°C/350°F/gas mark 4. Cut the dough into very thin slices with a sharp knife. Place them on a lined baking tray and bake for six to seven minutes. (You will need to bake in batches.) Watch them, as they burn easily. Cool on a wire rack, then store in an airtight tin for up to five weeks.

YOU WILL NEED
250g salted butter
125g golden syrup
250g dark muscovado sugar
50g blanched almonds, chopped
50g finely chopped candied
    lemon zest
50g finely chopped candied
    orange zest
1 tbsp ground cinnamon
2 tsp ground cloves
½ tsp ground cardamom
½ tsp ground ginger
500g plain flour, sifted

Hallon cookies *Makes 20 hearts and 20 rounds*

My friend, food writer Alice Brax, sent me a box of these. I've dreamt of them since! This was her recipe, but I've adapted it.

Mix the flour, potato flour, sugar, baking powder and salt in a bowl. Split the vanilla pod lengthways and scrape out the seeds into the bowl. Add the butter and half the egg. Rub with your fingertips until the dough forms a ball. Refrigerate for one hour.

Preheat the oven to 200°C/400°F/gas mark 6. Place the dough between sheets of baking parchment and roll out until 1cm thick. Peel off the top layer and cut out hearts with a 5cm cutter and rounds with a 4cm cutter. Take half of each shape, and cut out smaller hearts and rounds. Take the shapes with the holes and paint them with egg on the undersides, before pressing them on to the whole shapes. Fill the holes with jam. Put on lined baking trays and brush with the remaining egg. Bake for 10–12 minutes, then cool on a wire rack. Store in an airtight tin for up to two weeks.

YOU WILL NEED
225g plain flour, sifted
60g potato flour, sifted
100g caster sugar
1 tsp baking powder
pinch of salt
1 vanilla pod
200g cold salted butter,
    cut into small pieces
1 egg, beaten
100–150ml raspberry jam

'There are many versions of brown cookies. This is my mother's recipe.'

GIFTS FROM THE KITCHEN

I make jams, chutneys, jellies and vinegars for myself, but I also give them as presents. At Christmas, whenever I am invited to a party or for dinner, I bring jars and bottles of homemade preserves with me for my hosts. Sometimes, I suspect that my friends only invite me for dinner when they run out of jam and chutney... but I take it as a compliment!

You may think that making edible gifts is too time consuming but, really, in a weekend you can get a lot done, and most of the recipes blip away on the stove taking care of themselves while you get on with other things. You can also use preserving as an excuse to catch up with family members; when certain fruits and vegetables are in season, for instance, I go to visit my mother and cook with her at her home in the country.

I think these edible presents are very personal. You have taken the time and effort to make something special for people you care about. These gifts can't be bought, in a world where everything is for sale...

❄ CHRISTMAS CHUTNEY ❄ APPLE CHUTNEY ❄ APPLE JELLY ❄ REDCURRANT JELLY ❄ ROSEHIP CHUTNEY
❄ LINGONBERRY COMPOTE ❄ RASPBERRY VINEGAR ❄ SEA BUCKTHORN VINEGAR ❄ BLACKCURRANT JAM
❄ GLØGG EXTRACT ❄ CHOCOLATE-DIPPED CANDIED ORANGES

> 'Homemade gløgg is always a lovely treat when it's cold outside.'

'A gift you make in
your own kitchen
is a real treasure
to receive at
Christmas.'

Christmas chutney

Makes 4 x 500ml jars

My daughter Michala – when she was about 10 years old – made this as a Christmas present for the family. She called it 'Christmas chutney'. However, she never cared to do it again, so I took over her recipe and idea! This is great with lamb or chicken dishes.

Peel and core the apples and stone the plums. Cut the apples, plums, tomatoes and onion quite finely. Place in a heavy-based saucepan with all the other ingredients, and bring to a boil.

Let the chutney simmer, uncovered, for 30–45 minutes, until it is as thick as jam, stirring frequently. When it's ready, pour the chutney into sterilised jars and seal. Stored in a dark, cool place, this will keep for months.

YOU WILL NEED
500g cooking apples
500g plums
500g tomatoes
1 red onion
100g raisins
1 red chilli, finely chopped
150g root ginger, finely chopped
1 cinnamon stick
5 cardamom pods
5 cloves
½ tbsp black peppercorns
100ml cider vinegar
500g caster sugar

Apple chutney *Makes 3 x 400ml jars*

I serve this with roast chicken or pork during the winter months. It is perfect eaten with slices of crisp pork belly, and is just a lovely thing to have in the cupboard to spice up any meal.

Rinse the apples, cut out the cores and cut the flesh into small cubes (keep the skins on). Place them in a heavy-based saucepan with the chillies, sultanas, cinnamon and vinegar. Bring to a boil, then add the sugar and stir until it dissolves.

Let the chutney simmer, uncovered, until it has become as thick as jam. Stir very often, as it can easily catch and burn on the pan. Pour into sterilised jars and seal. Stored in a dark, cool place, this will keep for months.

YOU WILL NEED
1.5kg Cox's Orange Pippin apples
4 green chillies, finely chopped
200g sultanas
1 cinnamon stick
100ml cider vinegar
300g demerara sugar

Apple jelly *Makes 5 x 200ml jars*

This versatile jelly can be used in cooking, or it goes with cheese, roast meat or even ice cream. In Scandinavia we eat it with roast and fried fish, too. It's also lovely with foie gras, if any French traditions sneak their way into your Christmas... To make it even more delicious, add 50–75ml of Calvados just before it thickens.

YOU WILL NEED
2kg Belle de Boskoop apples, or other firm, tart apples
800g caster sugar per 1 litre of apple juice

Cut the apples, with skin and cores, into pieces, put in a heavy-based pan with 200ml of water and bring to a boil. Cover and simmer for 45 minutes; don't stir. Pour into a jelly bag over a bowl and leave overnight. Don't squeeze the bag, or it will be cloudy.

Next day, measure the juice, add the sugar and bring to a boil, stirring until the sugar dissolves. Let it boil, uncovered, over a medium heat, until drops of the juice set on a chilled plate. Skim off any scum and pour into sterilised jars. Seal the next day, so the steam can escape overnight. Stored in a dark, cool place, this keeps for months.

Redcurrant jelly *Makes 4 x 200ml jars*

Crucial for Christmas, used in Special Gravy (see page 112), and also eaten with duck and goose. I always have it in my cupboard.

YOU WILL NEED
1kg redcurrants
850g caster sugar per 1 litre of redcurrant juice

Rinse the currants, leaving them on their stalks but removing any coarser stems. Place them in a heavy-based saucepan with 50ml of water and bring to a boil. Allow to simmer until the currants burst. Pour them into a jelly bag and leave to drain overnight. Don't press the bag, or the jelly will be cloudy.

Measure the juice, pour it into a saucepan and bring to a boil. Add the sugar, stirring until it dissolves. Let the jelly simmer, uncovered, until it has thickened. You'll know when this is, because drops of the juice thicken on the spoon and drop back only slowly into the jelly. Turn off the heat and carefully skim off any scum, then pour the jelly into sterilised jars. Seal the next day (to allow all the steam to escape overnight). Stored in a dark, cool place, this keeps for months.

Rosehip chutney _Makes 3 x 500ml jars_

Pick rosehips in August beside the seaside, rinse and freeze them, then use them to make chutney and jam all through the winter. Because picking and deseeding rosehips is hard, time-consuming work, this chutney is a treasured gift among my friends.

Cut the rosehips in half and remove the seeds with a teaspoon (it's a good idea to use disposable gloves, as the seeds cause itching). Rinse the hips in cold water and leave to drain in a colander. Cut them into small pieces with a knife, or in a food processor.

Combine the rosehips, onion and chillies in a heavy-based saucepan with all the other ingredients and 300ml of water and bring to a boil, stirring to dissolve the sugar. Let the chutney simmer, uncovered, until it is as thick as jam, stirring frequently (it can take as much as 30–40 minutes). Pour into sterilised jars and seal. Stored in a dark, cool place, this will keep for months.

> **YOU WILL NEED**
> 1kg rosehips
> 1 large onion, chopped
> 2 red chillies, finely sliced
> 100ml cider vinegar
> 300g caster sugar
> 1 tsp salt
> 1 tbsp whole peppercorns

Lingonberry compote

Makes 4 x 250ml jars

An important source of vitamin C, which is probably the reason this is such a vital part of the Scandinavian food culture. Very versatile, use this to bake a pie, to accompany meat and fish, or with cheese on toasted rye bread in the morning. It's worth looking for frozen lingonberries online, but you can substitute cranberries.

If using fresh berries, rinse them in cold water and leave them to drain in a colander. (You don't need to rinse frozen berries.) Place the berries in a heavy-based saucepan with 200ml of water, bring to a boil and cook, uncovered, for 10 minutes.

Add the sugar and return to a boil for 10 minutes. Skim the surface, pour into sterilised jars and seal. Stored in a dark, cool place, this will keep for one month.

> **YOU WILL NEED**
> 1kg lingonberries, fresh or frozen
> 600g caster sugar

Raspberry vinegar *Makes 1 litre*

One of my favourite vinegars, for salad dressings, pouring over ice cream or adding to a cake icing. I also use it for seasoning sauces.

Carefully rinse the raspberries in cold water, then leave them to drain in a colander. Dissolve the sugar in the vinegar. Place the raspberries in a two-litre sterilised jar and pour over the sweet vinegar. Seal the jar and leave in a light place – a windowsill is perfect – for four weeks or more.

Pour the raspberries into a jelly bag over a bowl to drain for some hours, or overnight. (Don't squeeze the bag or the vinegar will be cloudy.) Pour the vinegar into sterilised bottles and seal. Stored in a dark, cool place, the vinegar will keep for years.

YOU WILL NEED
500g raspberries
50g caster sugar
1 litre white wine vinegar

Sea buckthorn vinegar

Makes 700ml

Make this when the bright orange-yellow berries are in season, then store it for Christmas. It's lovely on salads, with fish, or with baked root vegetables. Sea buckthorn is common all across Europe and as far as north west China, and I'm astonished other nations don't make more of the berries, as it's so easy to forage your own.

If the berries are fresh, rinse them in cold water two or three times. Leave to drain in a colander. (If you're using frozen berries, you don't have to rinse them.) Mix the vinegar and sugar in a saucepan with 200ml of water and heat until the sugar dissolves. Cool completely. Place the berries in a two-litre sterilised jar and pour over the sweet vinegar. Seal the jar and leave in a light place – a windowsill is perfect – for four weeks or more.

Pour the berries into a jelly bag over a bowl, leaving them to drain for some hours, or overnight. (Don't squeeze the bag.) Bottle, seal and store as above.

YOU WILL NEED
200g sea buckthorn berries, fresh or frozen
500ml white wine vinegar
250g caster sugar

'I make vinegars
when the berries
are in season,
and store them
for Christmas.'

Blackcurrant jam *Makes 5 x 250ml jars*

YOU WILL NEED
1kg blackcurrants
1kg caster sugar

I eat a lot of jam but I don't much like shop-bought versions; they tend to have too much sugar and too little fruit. At the weekends, we eat jam for breakfast with bread and cheese, or with pancakes, after our porridge. We go through a lot of jam in a year, especially during the long Christmas holiday.

Rinse the currants and remove the stalks. Put them in a big bowl and prick them with a fork. Mix in the sugar, cover with a tea towel and leave at room temperature for two to three hours, or overnight.

Place the mixture in a heavy-based saucepan and slowly bring to a boil. Let it boil for eight to 10 minutes, but make sure it doesn't catch and burn. Skim the surface, then pour into sterilised jars and seal. Stored in a dark, cool place, this keeps for months.

Gløgg extract *Makes 2 x 250ml bottles: 1 bottle is enough for 1 quantity (8 glasses) of Gløgg (see page 61).*

YOU WILL NEED
200ml blackcurrant juice
75ml lemon juice
20 cloves
10 cardamom pods, lightly crushed
2 x 5–6cm cinnamon sticks
200g caster sugar

Most people in Scandinavia just buy ready-made versions of this; they are fine but a bit too sweet for my taste and lack the spices. This means that everyone's gløgg tastes the same and, as you are offered a glass everywhere in December, by the end of the month it's a relief to taste something like this, that's more interesting.

Place all the ingredients in a saucepan with 300ml of water. Cover and bring to a boil, stirring to help the sugar dissolve. Simmer for 30 minutes, then drain through a nylon sieve.

Discard the spices and pour the liquid into sterilised bottles. Seal at once. Stored in a dark, cool place, this keeps for months.

Chocolate-dipped candied oranges

Makes 20 whole slices, or 40 half-moon slices

Oranges and chocolate are a deservedly classic combination. When you make candied oranges, they develop an even more intense flavour.

YOU WILL NEED
750g caster sugar
500g slices of organic orange,
    halved if you prefer
about 200g Tempered Chocolate
    (see page 22)

Put the sugar in a heavy-based saucepan with 500ml of water. Bring to a boil, stirring to help the sugar dissolve, then boil until the syrup reaches 110–115°C on a sugar thermometer.

Add the fruit to the syrup, reduce the heat and let simmer very gently for five minutes. Take the fruit out of the syrup and let it dry on a wire rack while you preheat the oven to 180°C/350°F/gas mark 4. Dry the orange slices further in the oven for 10 minutes, then let them cool down.

Dip each slice in tempered chocolate and leave to set on a wire rack. Store in an airtight container for up to two weeks.

ADVENT: A WHOLE MONTH OF CHRISTMAS

Advent starts on the fourth Sunday before Christmas, so the first Advent Sunday falls between 27 November and 3 December. In Scandinavia, this time is part of the festivities, leading up to the big event on Christmas Eve.

Celebrate one of the Advent Sundays outside. Play in the snow: remember there is no such thing as bad weather, only the wrong clothes. Serve hot drinks, salmon sandwiches, and 'nisse' (elf) cake, make a stew and bake bread over the open fire; I'll show you how in the first part of this chapter.

We get together with family and friends indoors as well, as you'll see in the second part of this chapter, to prepare for all the parties in December, baking and making chocolates for Christmas. On the first Advent Sunday I also decorate my house and make a gingerbread town. Children visit, and make and decorate their own cookies. In the evening we eat apple æbleskiver 'doughnuts' and drink gløgg.

ADVENT OUTDOORS: ❄ **OPEN SALMON SANDWICH ON RUIS BREAD** ❄ **LAMB STEW** ❄ **ELDERBERRY AND RUM TODDY** ❄ **ELDERBERRY CORDIAL** ❄ **HOT ELDERFLOWER DRINK** ❄ **'NISSE' CAKE** ❄ **CHRISTMAS PORRIDGE**
ADVENT INDOORS: ❄ **APPLE ÆBLESKIVER** ❄ **GLØGG** ❄ **CHOCOLATES: MARZIPAN AND NOUGAT; MARZIPAN WITH COGNAC AND WALNUTS; SALTED POPCORN** ❄ **PEPPER COOKIES** ❄ **GINGERBREAD TOWN**

'Make sure your household "nisse" (elf) is happily fed all through December.'

'In our street we meet every day in December to drink something hot and sing Christmas carols.'

Open salmon sandwich on ruis bread *Makes 12*

I always feel there has to be something salty in between all the sweet things, so this is perfect. You can use ready-made rye crispbread instead of homemade Ruis (see page 78), if you're not a baker.

YOU WILL NEED
1 small bunch of dill
200g cream cheese
1 cucumber
1 Ruis loaf (see page 78),
    or 12 pieces of crisp bread
12 slices of smoked salmon

Finely chop the dill, leaving a few sprigs to serve, and mix well with the cream cheese. Cut the cucumber into thin slices.

If using a Ruis loaf, cut it in two halves and then into thin slices.

Spread the cream cheese mix on the bread, followed by two or three slices of cucumber. Place a slice of smoked salmon on top and add a sprig of dill.

'Somebody left their boot out in the snow... see what the "nisse" (elf) left in it!'

'A piping hot drink truly heats you up from within. It's such a delightful way to keep warm when out in the snow.'

Elderberry and rum toddy

Serves 8

This is a great alternative to Gløgg (see page 61), and I always serve it for one of my Advent Sunday gatherings.

Mix the elderberry cordial with 1 litre of water and the cloves. Bring to a boil, add the raisins and almonds, reduce the heat and simmer for five minutes. Remove from the heat and add the rum. Serve very hot, in glasses.

Elderberry cordial

Makes about 1.5 litres

You can buy elderflower cordial everywhere, and loads of people make it... so why not elderberry? It's delicious.

Put the berries and apples in a pan, add 500ml of water, bring to a boil, then simmer until the berries burst. Line a nylon sieve with muslin and pour the mixture through into a bowl. Pour the juice into a clean pan and bring to a boil, add the sugar and boil for two to three minutes. Skim the surface. Pour into sterilised bottles. Store in a dark, cool place for up to six months. When opened, keep in the refrigerator.

Hot elderflower drink *Serves 8*

A hot drink for children, this is lovely and comforting.

Mix the homemade cordial with 1 litre of water, or a shop-bought cordial according to the instructions on the bottle. Mix with the almonds and sultanas in a saucepan and bring to a boil. Remove from the heat and serve very hot, in glasses.

'Nisse' (elf) cake *Makes about 24 pieces*

A speciality from the Island of Funen, where my family is from. Form it into any shape, but it's best eaten on the day it is made.

Melt the butter for the dough in a saucepan, add the milk and cool to lukewarm. Dissolve the yeast in the milk, add the eggs and stir. Add the flour, sugar and salt. Knead on a floured work surface until smooth and elastic. Put the dough in a bowl, cover with a damp tea towel and leave to rise for 1½ hours at room temperature.

For the topping, melt the butter and sugar in a saucepan until boiling, stirring constantly. Cool to room temperature. Form the dough into a 'nisse', or other shape, then place it on a baking tray lined with baking parchment and spread the filling on top, leaving the edges free. Cover with cling film and leave to rise for 30 minutes.

Preheat the oven to 200°C/400°F/gas mark 6. Bake the cake in the hot oven for about 25 minutes. Leave to cool on the tray, then let the children loose to decorate!

YOU WILL NEED
For the dough
100g salted butter
250ml whole milk
50g fresh yeast (or 19g dried yeast if you really have to!)
2 eggs, beaten
500g plain flour, sifted, plus more to dust
2 tbsp caster sugar
½ tsp salt

For the caramel topping
150g salted butter
150g soft dark brown sugar

Christmas porridge
Serves 8 (or 4 with leftovers for Sweet Rice Pancakes, see page 82)

The 'nisse' (elf) lives where we can't see him. He is naughty, and the best way to stay friends with him is to leave porridge in the attic for him, with lots of butter, sugar and cinnamon! Then, he won't eat your cookies, or hide your favourite things; instead he will leave little presents in your boots.

Pour 500ml of water into a heavy-based saucepan and bring to a boil. Add the rice and let it boil for two minutes, stirring. Add the milk and return to a boil, still stirring. Cover, reduce the heat to low and simmer for 45 minutes, stirring occasionally. Remove from the heat and add the salt. Mix the sugar and cinnamon in a small bowl. Serve the porridge in warm dishes. Make a dent with a spoon in the middle of each and add a spoonful of butter. Sprinkle generously with the cinnamon sugar.

YOU WILL NEED
For the porridge
500g short-grain pudding rice
2 litres whole milk
2 tsp salt

To serve
100g caster sugar
2 tbsp ground cinnamon
50g salted butter

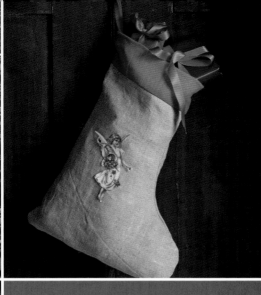

'You start a present calendar on 1 December and there is a present every day. I get an Advent present from my husband each Sunday at breakfast.'

'Benjamin and Elvira are baking and decorating cookies with Kelly. It is not difficult, and the best fun is when you use coloured icings.'

'Æbleskiver are a special December treat... I only cook them at Christmas.'

Apple æbleskiver *Serves 8*

My aunt Sarah was from the small island of Ærø, where my father was born and my grandfather lived all his life. She was the only member of my family that made these æbleskiver, which are like light doughnuts with a nice sour surprise in the centre. I'm afraid you'll need a special pan, but you can buy it easily online.

Dissolve the yeast in the milk in a large bowl. In another mixing bowl, sift together the flour, salt and cardamom. Slit the vanilla pods lengthways, scrape out the seeds with the tip of a knife and add them to the dry ingredients with the sugar. Whisk the eggs yolks into the milk mixture. Add the dry ingredients and beat to make a dough. In a separate bowl, whisk the egg whites until stiff, then fold them into the dough. Leave to stand for 40 minutes.

Peel and core the apples and cut into 1cm cubes. Heat the æbleskiver pan over a medium heat. Put a little butter in each indentation and, when it has melted, pour in some of the batter. Place a piece of apple in each and cook for three to five minutes, or until golden underneath, then turn the doughnuts over. Continue frying for about four to five minutes or until golden, then remove from the pan. Repeat with the remaining batter. Dust with icing sugar and serve immediately with raspberry jam.

YOU WILL NEED
40g fresh yeast (or 15g dried yeast if you really have to!)
800ml lukewarm whole milk
600g plain flour
2½ tsp salt
1½ tsp ground cardamom
2 vanilla pods
3 tbsp caster sugar
4 eggs, separated
2 apples
100–150g salted butter

To serve
icing sugar
raspberry jam

Gløgg *Makes 8 glasses*

Everybody serves gløgg in December in Scandinavia, so this is when you really appreciate a homemade, not-too-sweet version.

Combine the wine, Gløgg Extract, almonds and raisins in a saucepan. Heat for 10 minutes over a low heat, without boiling.

Serve in glasses, with teaspoons for catching the raisins and almonds.

YOU WILL NEED
750ml bottle of red wine
250ml Gløgg Extract (see page 43)
150g blanched almonds, coarsely chopped
150g raisins

Chocolate marzipan and nougat *Makes about 25*

You'll need soft Danish nougat for this, as you need to be able to roll it out. Get it at danishfooddirect.co.uk or scandikitchen.co.uk.

Cut the marzipan into three pieces. Roll out one piece on a work surface dusted with icing sugar to about 5mm thick. Halve the soft nougat and roll out one piece on top of the rolled marzipan to cover it. Roll out the second piece of marzipan as before and lay it on top of the nougat, followed by the remaining nougat. Roll out the final piece of marzipan and lay it on the stack, so that you have five layers of alternating marzipan and nougat. (If you prefer, you can make just three thicker layers, as we did for the photo.)

Slice the stack into 1cm diamonds and dip them in tempered chocolate. Let them rest on a wire rack until the chocolate has set.

YOU WILL NEED
400g marzipan
icing sugar, to dust
200g soft Danish nougat
about 150g Tempered Chocolate, to cover (see page 22)

Chocolate marzipan with cognac and walnuts *Makes about 20*

You can make endless variations on this theme: replace the walnuts with prunes, orange zest, dates or raisins, or substitute any other liqueur you like for the cognac.

Mix the marzipan, cognac, walnuts and nougat well, then form the mixture into little balls, each about the volume of a teaspoon. Dip them in the tempered chocolate, then let them rest on a wire rack until the chocolate has set.

YOU WILL NEED
300g marzipan
4 tbsp cognac
75g walnuts, chopped
75g soft Danish nougat
about 150g Tempered Chocolate, to cover (see page 22)

Chocolate salted popcorn *Makes 450g*

I started making this when my children were small. Over the years, I have learned to make a double portion every time, because a lot of it is eaten before it ever leaves the kitchen...

YOU WILL NEED
2 tbsp corn oil
150g popcorn kernels
salt
about 500g Tempered Chocolate,
   to cover (see page 22)

Heat the oil in a large pot and add the popcorn. Cover with a lid and reduce the heat. Wait for the kernels to pop; when the pot goes silent, they are done. Uncover, pour the popcorn into a large bowl and sprinkle with salt, then leave to cool.

When cool, mix in the tempered chocolate and put on a tray lined with baking parchment. Leave to set for about 30 minutes.

Break into pieces. Use them to fill cellophane bags, tied with coloured ribbon, or serve in bowls at a party.

Pepper cookies *Makes 30–50, depending on size*

Fun for children to make, these 'pepparkakor' can be decorated with icing in many colours. Hang as decorations, or just eat them!

YOU WILL NEED

For the dough
150ml golden syrup
250ml dark soft brown sugar
2 tbsp ground ginger
2 tsp ground cinnamon
½ tsp ground cloves
175g salted butter, softened
150ml double cream
½ tsp bicarbonate of soda
750g plain flour, plus more to dust

For the icing
300g icing sugar
selection of food colours

Mix the syrup, sugar, spices and butter in a big mixing bowl, beating until soft and smooth. Then add the cream and mix again. Sift together the bicarbonate of soda and flour, then mix into the butter mixture.

Flour a work surface and knead the dough well, then wrap in cling film and leave to rest in the refrigerator overnight.

When ready to bake, preheat the oven to 200°C/400°F/gas mark 6. Roll out the dough really thinly on a floured surface and cut out with cookie cutters, using different shapes and sizes. Place on baking trays lined with baking parchment and bake for about eight minutes. Leave to cool on a wire rack.

Divide the icing sugar between small bowls and add different food colours, then add water a little bit at a time, until the icing is smooth (make sure it doesn't get too runny). When the cookies are cold, decorate with the icing.

'The best
thing is all the
nibbling while
you ice the
cookies.'

Gingerbread town *Makes a medium-sized town*

Here is a fun and easy way to make a gingerbread decoration. It can be difficult to make a house, especially for small children, so this is a great solution. The only borders to your gingerbread town are your imagination! You can make anything: houses, trees, cars, or even a castle.

YOU WILL NEED

For the dough
150g dark soft brown sugar
250g golden syrup
150g salted butter
1 tsp ground ginger
3 tsp ground cinnamon
½ tsp ground cloves
2 tsp bicarbonate of soda
1 egg, beaten
550g plain flour, sifted,
    plus more to dust
1 piece of cardboard

For the icing
1 egg white
125g icing sugar
selection of food colours

Melt the sugar, syrup and butter in a saucepan. Add the spices and bicarbonate of soda and stir well. Cool the mixture, then mix in the egg and flour. Wrap in cling film and allow to rest for one hour in the fridge.

Draw the figures you would like to have – a tree, house, car, 'nisse' (elf) – and cut them out of the cardboard to make templates.

Preheat the oven to 200°C/400°F/gas mark 6.

Roll the dough out on a floured surface to about 5mm thick. Place your templates on the dough and cut out the gingerbread with a small sharp knife. If you want to hang them up, make a hole in each with a pencil. Place on a baking tray lined with baking parchment and bake for eight minutes. Leave to cool on a wire rack.

For the icing, mix the egg white and icing sugar, divide between small bowls and add different food colours. Form piping bags from pieces of baking parchment and fill them with icing, then use them to decorate the pieces of gingerbread. Leave until the icing is dry before hanging up your little gingerbread decorations, if you want.

'You could decorate your whole house with iced gingerbread trees and snowmen.'

FESTIVE BRUNCH

There are many different ways to celebrate the four Advent Sundays in Scandinavia. Mainly, it's about getting together and celebrating the end of the year and... well... life! You can choose the way you want to mark every Sunday, and each Scandinavian family has their own traditions.

Serving brunch on an Advent Sunday, just before going to the woods to pick out a Christmas tree, is a great way to spend the day. This is a new ritual I've started now my children are grown up and aren't around every day. We get together to eat brunch, then set out to buy and decorate the tree. When that's finished, we nibble on leftovers and watch 'Love Actually' and 'White Christmas'.

❄ BEETROOT-HORSERADISH CURED SALMON ❄ KALE SALAD WITH JERUSALEM ARTICHOKES
❄ BAKED OMELETTE WITH SPINACH ❄ ROOT VEGETABLE SALAD ❄ RUIS BREAD
❄ CHRISTMAS DANISH PASTRIES ❄ SWEET RICE PANCAKES WITH BLUEBERRY COMPOTE

'I become pathetically happy when I unwrap my Christmas things and start to decorate my house.'

'Fly to the North Pole on a goose to visit Father Christmas.'

Beetroot-horseradish cured salmon *Serves 16–20*

Cured salmon is a big part of Scandinavian food culture and very easy to do. The beetroot gives a beautiful colour and a sweet, earthy taste. It's lovely for brunch, and goes well with the salad below. You can freeze any leftovers... not that they're likely!

In a bowl, mix together the beetroot, horseradish, salt, sugar, peppercorns and fennel seeds. Place the salmon, skin side down, in a non-reactive dish, pour the beetroot cure over and cover with cling film. Put the dish in the fridge for three days.

Rinse off the beetroot mixture and wipe the fish clean. To serve, slice as you would a side of smoked salmon, leaving the skin behind.

YOU WILL NEED
200g peeled, grated beetroot
200g peeled, grated fresh horseradish
200g coarse salt
300g caster sugar
2 tbsp black peppercorns, crushed
2 tbsp fennel seeds
2kg side of salmon, with skin

Kale salad with Jerusalem artichokes *Serves 6*

A modern salad... but with a very traditional dressing. I think this was more or less the only dressing my grandmother used, though she would add vinegar where I use lemon.

Rinse the kale in cold water and leave to drain in a colander. Gently squeeze the leaves to remove as much water as possible, without crushing them.

Rinse the Jerusalem artichokes, scrub well, and cut into very thin slices, using a mandolin if you have one. Mix the kale and the Jerusalem artichokes. Mix the cream, sugar and lemon juice and zest and immediately pour it over the vegetables, tossing well, so the Jerusalem artichokes don't discolour. Check for seasoning, and serve.

YOU WILL NEED
300g kale, trimmed, thick stalks removed
150g Jerusalem artichokes
250ml double cream
2 tbsp caster sugar
juice of 1 unwaxed lemon and finely grated zest of ½
salt
freshly ground black pepper

'Salmon and kale
are integral tastes
of the festive season
in Scandinavia.'

'Always try to
cook food which
has a rainbow of
lovely colours.'

Baked omelette with spinach *Serves 6*

You've got to have eggs for brunch, and here they are baked with winter spinach. Serve, in wedges, with fried bacon on the side.

Preheat the oven to 175°C/350°F/gas mark 4.

Rinse the spinach in plenty of cold water, then leave to drain in a colander. Put into a saucepan over a high heat and cover. Steam for two minutes, then drain through a colander and squeeze the leaves to remove as much water as possible.

Beat the eggs well, add the cream, nutmeg, salt and pepper and beat again.

Oil an ovenproof dish with the olive oil. Place the spinach in the dish, then pour over the egg mixture. Bake in the oven for about 30 minutes, or until set and quite firm (check by piercing with a knife). Cut into squares or wedges to serve.

YOU WILL NEED
800g fresh spinach
12 organic eggs
50ml single cream
½ tsp freshly grated nutmeg
salt
freshly ground black pepper
1 tbsp olive oil

Root vegetable salad *Serves 6*

A lovely crunchy salad with a lot of flavours. In Scandinavia, we eat a lot of root vegetables in the winter. This is nice with Ruis (see overleaf) and salmon, or as part of the Christmas smörgåsbord.

Preheat the oven to 180°C/350°F/gas mark 4.

Peel the beetroots and parsnips, wash the Jerusalem artichokes and scrub them well, then cut all the vegetables into even chunks. Place in an ovenproof dish and mix with the oil, salt and pepper. Bake for 45 minutes, then remove and cool for 10 minutes.

Whisk all the ingredients for the dressing together and mix with the root vegetables. Season generously and serve warm or cold.

YOU WILL NEED
For the salad
300g yellow beetroots
300g purple beetroots
300g parsnips
300g Jerusalem artichokes
4 tbsp olive oil
salt
freshly ground black pepper

For the dressing
4 tbsp cider vinegar
2 tbsp Dijon mustard
2 tbsp honey
5 tbsp peeled, grated horseradish

Ruis bread *Makes 3 loaves*

A very dense rye bread perfect for breakfast, this should be eaten on the day it is baked, though any leftovers make lovely toast.

YOU WILL NEED
15g fresh yeast
950g wholemeal rye flour,
    plus more to dust
4 tsp sea salt flakes

Put the yeast in a large bowl with 200ml of lukewarm water and 4 tbsp of the flour. Stir well. Cover with a clean tea towel and leave in a warm place overnight.

Next day, mix in the salt and remaining flour with enough lukewarm water (about 800ml) to make a soft dough. Knead the dough on a floured surface for a few minutes; it will be soft and sticky, but you can still handle it with a lot of flour on your hands. Cover with a clean tea towel once more and leave to rise in a warm place for six hours. Do this just before going to bed, or first thing in the morning, depending on when you want to eat the bread.

Punch the dough ('knock it back'), then divide it into three and roll into balls on a floured surface. Flatten each into a big round wheel, making a hole in the middle. Transfer to baking trays lined with baking parchment. Cover with clean tea towels for a final time and leave to rest in a warm place for two hours.

When ready to bake, preheat the oven to 220°C/425°F/gas mark 7. Dust the bread with flour and bake in the hot oven for 30 minutes, or until nicely browned.

'Danish pastries taste heavenly, whether for morning or afternoon tea.'

Christmas Danish pastries

Makes 20–24

Homemade Danish pastries – as the world knows – are to die for.
I bake them for birthdays then, for Christmas, I make these, with
spices and candied and dried fruit. I love them fresh from the
oven, or toasted the next day and eaten with blue cheese.

YOU WILL NEED
50g fresh yeast
200ml whole lukewarm milk
2 eggs, lightly beaten, plus 1 more
  to brush
100g caster sugar
½ tsp salt
400g plain flour, sifted,
  plus more to dust
½ tsp ground cinnamon
½ tsp ground coriander
½ tsp ground cardamom
150g raisins
80g candied lemon zest
80g candied orange zest
300g cold salted butter,
  thinly sliced

In a mixing bowl, dissolve the yeast in the milk. Stir in the 2 eggs, the sugar and salt.

In a separate large bowl, combine the flour, spices and raisins, candied lemon and orange zest (or use 160g candied mixed peel, if that's all you can find). Add the egg mixture, then stir until the dough comes together and leaves the edge of the bowl. Turn it on to a floured work surface and knead for five minutes, until shiny but not sticky. Return it to the bowl, cover with cling film and leave to rise in the refrigerator for 15 minutes.

Now roll out the dough into a 50cm square. Spread the slices of butter over the dough, about 10cm in from the edge, so that the square of dough has a smaller square of butter on top. Fold the edges of the dough over the butter so that they meet in the centre, making a smaller square parcel.

Carefully roll the dough into a 40x60cm rectangle, making sure it doesn't crack and that the butter stays inside the parcel.

Next you want to fold the dough so that the butter becomes layered within it. Fold the bottom third of dough over the middle third, and fold the top third down over that, as if folding a letter. Roll out the dough again and fold into three in the same way. Repeat three times, resting the dough in the fridge between rolls.

Finally, roll out the dough and cut out 20–24 squares. Take each one and press all the corners together. Place, corners down, on a baking tray lined with baking parchment. Cover with a clean tea towel and leave to rise for 30 minutes at room temperature. Preheat the oven to 220°C/425°F/gas mark 7. Brush the pastries with a little beaten egg and bake them for 12–15 minutes, then leave to cool on a wire rack.

Sweet rice pancakes with blueberry compote *Makes 16*

A classic leftovers dish, which I ate often as a child, this is utterly delicious. I think of it as Scandinavian French toast.

YOU WILL NEED

For the blueberry compote
500g blueberries, fresh or frozen
1 vanilla pod
100g caster sugar
juice from ½ organic orange and
    1 tsp of finely grated zest

For the pancakes
600ml cold Christmas Porridge
    (see page 57)
4–5 tbsp plain flour
2 eggs
1 tbsp caster sugar
finely grated zest of
    ½ unwaxed lemon
pinch of salt
30g salted butter

First make the compote. Rinse the berries, if fresh, and leave to drain. (Frozen berries don't need to be rinsed.) Split the vanilla pod lengthways and remove the seeds with the tip of a knife. Mix the berries, vanilla seeds, vanilla pod, sugar, orange juice and zest in a saucepan. Bring to a boil, then reduce the heat and simmer for 15 minutes, stirring occasionally. Pour the compote into a bowl. Stored in the fridge, it will keep for some weeks.

For the pancakes, mix the rice porridge and flour then beat in the eggs, one at a time. Add the sugar, lemon zest and salt and mix well. The batter will be rather thick.

Melt a little of the butter in a non-stick frying pan. Add 1 tbsp of the batter and fry until golden, then turn the pancake and fry it until golden on the other side. Keep warm, and repeat until all the batter has been used.

Serve the pancakes warm with the blueberry compote.

'After a brisk morning walk in the snow, these pancakes are the perfect comfort food.'

CHRISTMAS PARTY

We don't have a long tradition of Christmas parties in Scandinavia, as the festive season was always more of a family affair. That is changing fast, and the old rituals are taking on new and livelier forms.

I like to invite friends for a party on the Saturday before Christmas Eve, serve cocktails, champagne and canapés, and dance until early morning.

No children are allowed! This is our night to let loose with good friends before a whole two weeks closeted with our nearest and dearest.

❄ SALTED COD AND KALE PESTO ON CELERIAC BRUSCHETTA ❄ ELDERFLOWER CORDIAL ❄ KALE BRUSCHETTA
❄ LINGONBERRY GIN FIZZ ❄ LINGONBERRY CORDIAL ❄ MINI ROOT VEGETABLE CAKES WITH HORSERADISH CREAM
❄ 'BLUE CHRISTMAS' ❄ LIGHTLY SALTED DUCK WITH JERUSALEM ARTICHOKE CRISPS
❄ APPLE SAUCE WITH CRISPY PORK BELLY ❄ RING CAKE

'For Christmas parties, I make classic Scandinavian dishes into canapés.'

' "Hygge" is when we all get together, light candles, eat and drink. It wouldn't be "hyggeligt" without the food and drink.'

Salted cod and kale pesto on celeriac bruschetta *Serves 8*

In Sweden and Norway they serve lutefisk, which is salted cod or ling prepared using lye, and it's something of an acquired taste... It's never been part of my Christmas tradition, but I love salted fish so, instead, I've chosen this dish.

The day before you serve the dish, pour 500ml of water into a large pan with the sugar and salt for the fish, and bring to a boil. Cool, then add the cloves. Place the cod in a non-reactive dish and pour over the brine. Cover and refrigerate overnight.

For the celeriac, preheat the oven to 170°C/340°F/gas mark 3½. Cut off the roots of the celeriac, then carefully scrub. Dry it well. Brush with oil, then cover with salt. Bake until tender (about three hours). Cool, then slice and divide as if the celeriac were a loaf of bread that you were cutting for bruschetta.

Rinse the kale, then squeeze the leaves to remove as much water as possible. Shred coarsely. Place the kale, almonds, garlic, olive oil and lemon juice in a food processor and blend to a rough paste, seasoning to taste with more lemon, salt and pepper.

Remove the cod from the brine and dry it with kitchen paper. Cut into thin slices. Place some fish on a celeriac 'bruschetta' and top with the kale pesto.

YOU WILL NEED
For the fish
30g caster sugar
50g coarse sea salt
2 cloves
1kg cod fillets

For the baked celeriac
1 celeriac
2–3 tbsp olive oil
2–3 tbsp salt

For the kale pesto
100g kale leaves, ribs removed
40g blanched almonds
1 garlic clove, finely chopped
3 tbsp olive oil
2–3 tbsp lemon juice, or to taste
salt
freshly ground black pepper

Elderflower cordial *Makes 2.5 litres*

Add a drop of this to a champagne flute and top up with bubbly.

Put the flowers, lemons and citric acid into a very large heatproof bowl. Combine the sugar and 2 litres of water in a saucepan and bring to a boil, stirring until the sugar dissolves. Pour it over the flowers, cover with a tea towel and leave for four days.

Strain the mixture, pour into sterilised bottles and seal. Store in a cool, dark place.

YOU WILL NEED
40 elderflower clusters
3 unwaxed lemons, sliced
60g citric acid
1.5kg caster sugar

'A glass of champagne is always festive. Serve it with a drop of elderflower cordial.'

Kale bruschetta *Serves 8*

I love kale and use it as much as possible in season, so it's a big part of my Christmas cooking. This recipe is great with cocktails.

Rinse the kale in cold water. Squeeze the leaves to remove as much water as possible, then finely shred. Melt the butter for the bruschetta in a frying pan, add the bread, in batches if necessary, and fry on both sides until golden. Set aside. Add the butter for the kale to the same pan and sauté the leek and garlic for a few minutes, until softened but not browned. Add the kale and sauté for a further two or three minutes over a low heat. Remove from the heat and mix in the cheese. Divide the kale mixture between the bruschetta and serve with cocktails.

YOU WILL NEED
For the kale
300g kale leaves, ribs removed
25g salted butter
1 leek, rinsed and chopped
2 garlic cloves, finely chopped
150g Comté or Vesterhavs cheese, grated

For the bruschetta
25g salted butter
16 small slices of baguette

Lingonberry gin fizz *Serves 1*

You can scale this recipe up and serve it in a jug with crushed ice.

Place crushed ice in a cocktail shaker. Pour in the cordial and gin and shake. Add the sparkling water, then pour into a glass, holding back the ice. Squeeze in the lime.

YOU WILL NEED
3 tbsp Lingonberry Cordial (see below)
30ml gin
150ml sparkling water
1 wedge of lime

Lingonberry cordial *Makes 2 litres*

If you can't find lingonberries, use cranberries instead.

Place the berries and cardamom in a large pan, add 1.2 litres of water and bring to a boil. Reduce the heat, cover and simmer for 30 minutes. Pour into a jelly bag and drain over a large bowl (don't squeeze the bag or the cordial will be cloudy). Pour the liquid into a clean pan and return to a boil. Add the sugar and boil until it dissolves, skimming any scum. Pour into sterilised bottles and store in a dark, cool place.

YOU WILL NEED
2kg lingonberries, fresh or frozen
4 cardamom pods
700g caster sugar

Mini root vegetable cakes with horseradish cream

Serves 8

Perfect little mouth-watering bites. I've served these for years at winter parties and always get lots of compliments for them. They can be made the day before and reheated.

Peel the beetroots and parsnips and grate them. Mix all the ingredients except the oil and chervil well in a bowl, and let the mixture rest for one hour in the fridge.

Preheat the oven to 180°C/350°F/gas mark 4.

Form small, flat cakes from the beetroot mixture with your hands. Heat the oil in a frying pan and fry them on both sides until crisp, then place them in an ovenproof dish and roast in the oven for 20 minutes.

For the horseradish cream, mix the yogurt and crème fraîche in a bowl. Add the remaining ingredients and season to taste with sugar, salt and pepper.

Serve the root vegetable cakes with a spoonful of horseradish dressing, with a little more shredded horseradish and a chervil or flat leaf parsley leaf on top.

> **YOU WILL NEED**
> **For the cakes**
> 250g beetroots
> 250g parsnips
> 1 shallot, very finely chopped
> 50g blanched almonds, very finely chopped
> 2 tbsp finely chopped thyme
> 1 tsp ground coriander
> 100g rolled oats
> 3 eggs, lightly beaten
> salt
> freshly ground black pepper
> 1 tbsp olive oil
> chervil or flat leaf parsley leaves, to serve
>
> **For the horseradish cream**
> 100ml Greek yogurt
> 100ml full-fat crème fraîche
> 4 tbsp peeled, grated fresh horseradish, plus more to serve
> 2 tbsp lemon juice
> 1 tsp caster sugar, or to taste

'Blue Christmas' *Serves 1*

Sweet and fresh. You can replace the berries and cordial with any others you prefer. (See a photo of this drink on page 84.)

Put some ice cubes in a cocktail shaker with the cordial and vodka, and shake well. Fill a 300ml glass about one-third full with crushed ice and the frozen berries. Pour the vodka mixture into the glass and top up with the champagne to serve.

> **YOU WILL NEED**
> 30ml blueberry cordial
> 30ml vodka
> about 20 frozen blueberries
> about 50ml champagne or sparkling wine

Lightly salted duck with Jerusalem artichoke crisps *Serves 8*

We love to cure things in Scandinavia which, of course, comes from a long history of having to preserve food to survive. Now, we do it purely for taste and texture. This lightly cured duck also makes a delicious light lunch or starter; simply slice the cooked breasts and toss in a nut oil vinaigrette with salad leaves and walnuts.

YOU WILL NEED

For the brine
4 tbsp salt
4 tbsp caster sugar
2 bay leaves
6 cloves
finely grated zest of
    1 organic orange

For the duck
3 duck breasts

For the crisps
400g Jerusalem artichokes
2 tbsp olive oil
1 tbsp salt
freshly ground black pepper

Pour 800ml of water into a large pot and add all the ingredients for the brine. Place over a medium heat and stir until the salt and sugar have dissolved. Bring the brine to a boil, then turn off the heat and leave until completely cold. Place the duck breasts in a non-reactive dish and pour over the cold brine. Cover with cling film and put in the fridge overnight.

Preheat the oven to 180°C/350°F/gas mark 4.

Take the duck breasts out of the brine, dry them with kitchen paper and place in an ovenproof dish. Roast in the hot oven for 18 minutes; they should remain pink inside.

Wash the Jerusalem artichokes and cut them super-thin (if you have a mandolin, use that). Divide all the slices, keeping them in one layer, between two baking trays lined with baking parchment, then mix 1 tbsp of the olive oil into each trayful and sprinkle with salt and pepper. Bake in the oven at the same temperature as the duck for 25–30 minutes, or until they become crisp and golden. Cool on a wire rack.

Cut the duck breasts into cubes. Pierce a toothpick through the duck and thread the Jerusalem artichoke crisps on top, so each canapé looks like a small sailing boat.

Apple sauce with crispy pork belly *Serves 8*

This is mostly eaten in December, and long discussions can be held about how to cook it. In my family, we always serve pork belly with apple sauce, though others serve it with fried apples and onions. This is my family recipe and we call it 'Fynsk Æbleflæsk' to indicate the island where my family comes from. It's another recipe that, for me, just has to be part of Christmas.

YOU WILL NEED

For the pork
500g pork belly
4 slices rye bread, toasted
   and halved, to serve

For the apple sauce
1kg Cox's Orange Pippin apples
1 large onion, chopped
10 sprigs of thyme, plus more
   thyme leaves to serve
4 cloves
salt
freshly ground black pepper
lemon juice

Cut the meat into 2cm cubes and place them in a warm sauté pan. Fry until the fat has melted and the cubes are brown and crispy, stirring very often. Remove from the pan with a slotted spoon and drain on kitchen paper. Save 2–3 tbsp of the fat and discard the rest.

Peel and core the apples and cut them into cubes. Place the apples, onion, thyme and cloves into a saucepan and pour over the reserved fat. Bring to a boil, reduce the heat, cover and simmer over a low heat for about 20 minutes.

Mix the meat with the apple mixture and season to taste with salt, pepper and a little lemon juice. Sprinkle with thyme and serve with toasted rye bread.

Ring cake *Makes 1 big cake and about 36 cookies*

Good-quality marzipan is vitally important to this cake, which we call 'kransekage', and the taste will reflect the quality. The best marzipan contains 60 per cent almonds, with no artificial flavours or colours. These cakes are supposed to be soft in the centre, so take care not to over-bake them. It may be unusual to measure egg whites in a jug, but it's necessary here, as the volume of them is vital.

YOU WILL NEED

For the dough
150g almonds, with their skins
300g caster sugar
115ml egg whites
750g marzipan

For the small round cakes
12 hazelnuts
12 walnuts
12 small pieces of candied ginger

For the chocolate
300g Tempered Chocolate
(see page 22, use at least
60 per cent cocoa solids)

Whizz the almonds and sugar together in a food processor until finely ground. Add the egg whites and whizz again until the mixture has a smooth, white texture. Make sure it doesn't get too hot, or the egg whites will start to set. Grate the marzipan and blend it into the almond mixture. Transfer the mixture to a bowl, cover tightly with cling film and leave to rest in the fridge for a couple of hours, or overnight.

Preheat the oven to 175°C/350°F/gas mark 4.

Shape the mixture into nine sausages. Though each will be 2cm in diameter, they will differ in length by 3cm each. The longest should be 34cm, the others 31cm, 28cm, 25cm, 22cm, 19cm, 16cm, 13cm and 10cm respectively. Curl each piece into a ring, pressing to seal, and place them on a baking tray lined with baking parchment. Bake for 12–15 minutes, then leave to cool on a wire rack.

Roll the remaining dough into 10g balls. Press either a hazelnut, a walnut or a piece of candied ginger into each ball. Place these cookies on a baking tray lined with baking parchment and bake for about 10 minutes. Leave to cool on a wire rack.

One at a time, dip the top side of all the rings – except for the smallest – in tempered chocolate and place on top of each other, beginning with the biggest ring and ending with the smallest. You can make this one or two days ahead, if you need to, but no more.

Dip the bases of some of the cookies into melted chocolate and leave to set, upside down, on a wire rack. Store them in an airtight tin for up to two weeks.

THE CHRISTMAS EVE FEAST

Planning the Christmas Eve dinner is something I look forward to every year. I spend days writing and rewriting lists and brooding over which recipes to cook. Christmas Eve dinner is about family traditions, and my core recipes come from my mother and grandmother, but they are combined with my own, new rituals.

The main celebration in Scandinavia is on the evening of 24 December. We eat dinner, then we dance around the Christmas tree singing carols. Anybody who has seen Ingmar Bergman's movie 'Fanny and Alexander' will know how seriously we take the dancing. Finally it's time to open the presents, drink coffee and cognac, and eat all the tasty homemade cookies and chocolate.

In this chapter, I offer a selection of recipes that you can put together as a dinner, or as a buffet, but don't feel restricted by this particular, quite traditional Christmas Eve menu, or feel you can only eat it on 24 December! In Scandinavia, we eat specific meals on Christmas Eve and the days following. Most of the recipes for our festive dishes are in the book, but it's up to you to mix and match them, constructing your own menus for each different occasion.

❄ SLOW-ROAST DUCK ❄ TURNIP AND BACON GRATIN ❄ SLOW-COOKED GOOSE WITH APPLES AND PRUNES
❄ CURED LAMB CHOPS ❄ ROAST PORK WITH SPICES AND CRISP CRACKLING ❄ KALE SALAD WITH POMEGRANATE
❄ CARAMEL POTATOES ❄ WARM CHICORY SALAD ❄ RED CABBAGE ❄ SPECIAL GRAVY ❄ RED CABBAGE SALAD
❄ BRUSSELS SPROUTS WITH CLEMENTINES ❄ SPICED QUINCE HAM ❄ QUINCE SYRUP ❄ RICE PUDDING WITH HOT CHERRY SAUCE

'I set the table the same way every year. It's so reassuring that some things always stay the same.'

'The duck is roasting, the house is calm and beautiful, my family is here... this is when the magic begins.'

'Roasting the duck
is a big responsibility.
It must be crisp, yet
remain juicy.'

Slow-roast duck *Serves 8–10*

Always part of our Christmas dinner, I cook four to five, so I don't have to cook again until New Year! In our street, we line up all the barbecues and the men cook the birds, while they drink wine and beer. They are always in the Christmas spirit by dinner time...

Remove the giblets from the ducks and rinse them inside and out. If there is much fat inside, remove some of it, melt it and save it to use for crisp roast potatoes. Prepare a barbecue which has a lid.

For the stuffing, peel the celeriac and cut it into chunks. Melt the butter in a sauté pan and add the celeriac, shallots, parsley stalks and apricots. Sauté for five minutes. Add the brandy and sauté for five minutes more, then remove from the heat. Crush the allspice and stir it in with the 2 tsp of salt and a generous amount of pepper. Divide the stuffing in two and put one portion in each duck. Sew them closed with a trussing needle and kitchen string, then rub the ducks with salt and pepper.

Barbecue the birds for four to five hours, turning two or three times, then check if they are done: a probe thermometer in the thickest part of the thigh should read 80°C (175°F). Leave to rest for 10 minutes, then carve each bird into eight to 10 pieces.

YOU WILL NEED
2 ducks, each about 3.5kg

For the stuffing
400g celeriac
25g unsalted butter
2 shallots, roughly sliced
2 tbsp finely chopped parsley stalks
350g organic dried apricots, halved
50ml brandy
3 allspice berries
2 tsp salt
freshly ground black pepper

Turnip and bacon gratin
Serves 8

Traditional at Christmas in Scandinavia; mine is a rustic version.

If the turnips are big, halve or quarter them, but do not peel. Boil in salted water for 10–15 minutes, until just tender, then drain. Meanwhile, cut the bacon into cubes and fry in its own fat until golden. Preheat the oven to 200°C/400°F/gas mark 6.

Place the turnips in an ovenproof dish. Mix in the bacon and its fat. Bring the cream to a boil in a pan and simmer until it thickens, then add the nutmeg and salt and pepper. Stir this into the turnips and bake in the hot oven for 10 minutes.

YOU WILL NEED
1kg turnips, tops and bottoms cut off
salt
300g bacon, in one piece, or thickly sliced
200ml double cream
½ tsp freshly grated nutmeg
freshly ground black pepper

Slow-cooked goose with apples and prunes *Serves 5–6*

YOU WILL NEED
1 goose, about 5–6kg
1 litre cider

For the stuffing
4 apples, cored and cut
    into wedges
2 shallots, cut into wedges
leaves from 6 sprigs of thyme
200g whole prunes
1 tbsp salt
plenty of freshly ground pepper

My great grandmother lived in a small flat and didn't have a big enough oven for a goose. So, on the morning of 24 December, she would stuff the bird and go to the baker's shop. His ovens ran at 120°C (250°F), so he cooked all the geese for the neighbourhood for five or six hours. It gives a fantastic result: soft and juicy.

Remove the fat from the cavity, then dry the goose inside and out with kitchen paper. Preheat the oven to 120°C/250°F/gas mark ½. Mix the stuffing ingredients, stuff the goose and sew it shut with a trussing needle and kitchen string. Rub the bird with salt and put it in a roasting tin with half the cider.

Place the goose in the oven and cook for six hours, basting every 30 minutes with the juices. When they evaporate, use more of the cider. Start checking if the goose is done after five hours: a probe thermometer in the thickest part of the thigh should read 80°C (175°F). Increase the oven temperature to 225°C/440°F/gas mark 7½ for the last 10 minutes, so the skin crisps up. Leave to rest for 15 minutes, then carve.

Cured lamb chops *Serves 4*

YOU WILL NEED
1kg lamb chops
coarse salt

A Norwegian Christmas tradition, eat with potato-kohlrabi mash.

Place a layer of chops in a non-reactive container. Cover with salt. Add another layer of chops and salt and repeat to use all the chops. Cover and refrigerate for three days. Rinse the chops in cold water, place in a big bowl and fill it with cold water. Leave at room temperature for 24 hours, changing the water four or five times.

Place a wire rack on a trivet in a pot and pour water up to – not over – the rack. Bring to a boil, then reduce to a simmer. Lay the chops on the rack, cover and steam for three hours. Remove the chops and grill for a few minutes until brown, then serve.

'Slowly cooking
the goose at a low
temperature gives
the very best result.'

Roast pork with spices and crisp crackling *Serves 6*

I love this both on Christmas Eve and cold on Christmas Day, sliced on rye bread with a sprinkling of coarse salt and my Red Cabbage (see page 112). It's the kind of thing I will sneak out late at night to eat from the fridge all by myself, while I gaze at the cold weather outside and read a book, and my house is completely quiet.

Preheat the oven to 200°C/400°F/gas mark 6. Put the lemon zest in a mortar with the chilli, cardamom, garlic, cinnamon, star anise, salt and pepper. Grind with the pestle to a paste. (Or mix the ingredients to a paste in a mini food processor.) Remove the pork rind and fat in one piece from the top of the meat. Score a diamond pattern on the top surface of the meat, then rub in the spice mixture. Replace the piece of rind and fat, then tie all the way along the joint with a long piece of kitchen string at 2.5cm intervals. Place the pork in a roasting tin and roast for 1½ hours.

Remove from the oven and leave to rest for 15 minutes, then remove the string and carve the pork into slices. Serve, giving everyone a piece of the crisp crackling.

YOU WILL NEED
finely grated zest of
    1 unwaxed lemon
1 red chilli, chopped
seeds from 10 cardamom pods
5 garlic cloves, peeled and
    roughly chopped
5cm cinnamon stick,
    broken into pieces
2 star anise
salt
freshly ground black pepper
2kg boned pork foreloin, rind
    scored by your butcher

Kale salad with pomegranate *Serves 8*

One of the newer additions to our Christmas Eve dinner. The raw green taste of the kale amid all the sweet, fatty things is perfect.

Rinse the kale in cold water, then squeeze to remove the water. Shred the leaves finely. Cut the pomegranates in half and release the kernels and juice, discarding any white, pithy membrane. Mix the kale into the pomegranate kernels and juice. Mix the ingredients for the dressing and toss through the salad, seasoning to taste.

YOU WILL NEED
For the salad
400g kale leaves
3 pomegranates

For the dressing
juice of 1 lime
3 tbsp olive oil
salt
freshly ground pepper

'This is the kind of
thing I will sneak,
late at night, from
the fridge.'

Caramel potatoes *Serves 8*

Some people think this is a really weird way to eat potatoes!
In my family, they are an essential part of Christmas Eve dinner.
The secret to the perfect caramel potato is time; let them simmer
slow and easy while you turn them gently now and then, so they
are coated with caramel over and over again.

Boil the potatoes in salted water until tender. Peel them and leave to cool. (This can
be done the day before.) Place the peeled potatoes in a colander and pour cold water
over them. Leave them to drain well.

Melt the sugar over a very low heat in a big, heavy-based saucepan. Don't stir it!
When melted and golden brown, add the butter and let the mixture simmer until it
becomes a caramel, stirring as little as possible. Add the potatoes and gently turn
them in the caramel. Let them simmer at low heat for 35–40 minutes, turning often,
until they are coated in caramel on all sides. Serve.

YOU WILL NEED
2kg small potatoes
salt
300g caster sugar
175g salted butter, cut into pieces

Warm chicory salad *Serves 8*

Chicory is always part of the Christmas dinner, in Denmark we
actually called it 'Julesalat' or 'Christmas salad'. The bitter taste
is a very suitable foil to all the other dishes. I also make a simple
version with chicory, walnuts and grapes and a bit of walnut oil.

Cut each head of chicory into four long wedges. Melt the butter in a frying pan, add
the chicory wedges and fry them on all sides, then place them in a serving dish. Fry
the dates in the same frying pan for a few minutes, until they start to brown.

Arrange the dates, orange segments, orange zest and parsley over the chicory and
sprinkle with salt and pepper. Squeeze any juice that remains in the orange shells
over the salad, then serve.

YOU WILL NEED
6 heads of chicory
1 tsp salted butter
20 dates, stoned and chopped
    into strips
3 organic oranges, segmented,
    plus finely grated zest of 1
leaves from 2 sprigs of parsley
salt
freshly ground black pepper

Red cabbage *Serves 8*

This is part of the essential trinity of accompaniments to my Christmas Eve dinner, with Caramel Potatoes and Special Gravy (see page 111 and below). It can be made a week ahead, without the duck fat, and refrigerated. Reheat and add the fat to serve.

Melt the butter in a big saucepan and sauté the cabbage, turning, until shiny. Add all the remaining ingredients except the seasoning with 100ml of water. Cover and simmer for two hours. Finally, season generously with salt and pepper.

YOU WILL NEED
50g salted butter
2–2.5kg red cabbage, cored and shredded
1 onion, finely chopped
8 cloves
2 bay leaves
100g caster sugar
1 cinnamon stick
100ml blackcurrant cordial
1 tbsp duck fat
salt
freshly ground black pepper

Special gravy *Serves 8*

There has to be gravy. Each year when we sit down and eat dinner, my family tell me that the gravy has never tasted this good. When I cook it, I keep working on it until I think it's perfect, adding port, redcurrant jelly, cheese, salt and pepper. It's prepared with a lot of love. You should prepare the stock one or two days in advance.

To make the stock, peel the carrots, celeriac and onions and cut them into chunks. Fry the duck legs in a saucepan in their own fat, turning occasionally, until golden brown. Add all the other ingredients and bring to a boil with 1.5 litres of water. Reduce the heat and simmer, uncovered, for two to three hours. Strain the stock through a sieve. Cool and store in the fridge. Scrape off the fat that sets on top (save it for the Red Cabbage, above). There should be 1.2 litres of stock.

For the gravy, melt the butter in a saucepan. Whisk in the flour and cook until foaming and turning slightly brown. Add the stock a little at a time, stirring after each addition, until there are no lumps left. Slowly bring to a boil and add the port, blue cheese, redcurrant jelly, cream and pepper, stirring constantly. Leave to simmer for a few minutes and season to taste with salt and pepper. Adjust the colour with gravy browning, if you want. Reheat when ready to serve.

YOU WILL NEED
For the stock
2 carrots
200g celeriac
2 onions
2 duck legs
1 bottle of red wine
1 tbsp black peppercorns
4 bay leaves
1 tbsp coarse sea salt

For the gravy
75g salted butter
6 tbsp plain flour
100ml port
1 tsp Danish Blue cheese
1 tbsp redcurrant jelly
300ml double cream
freshly ground pepper
1 tsp gravy browning, or to taste (optional)

Red cabbage salad *Serves 8*

I often serve this as an alternative to hot vegetable dishes; it seems more modern somehow, and is wonderfully crunchy.

Remove and discard the core and the thick central ribs from the cabbage and finely shred the leaves. Cut the pears into wedges and mix with the cabbage. Roughly chop the walnuts and mix with the salad.

Whisk together all the ingredients for the dressing and mix it with the salad just before serving. Do not let the salad sit, because red cabbage goes soft very quickly.

YOU WILL NEED
For the salad
1 small red cabbage, about 600g
4 pears
150g walnuts

For the dressing
2 tbsp walnut oil
3 tbsp cider vinegar
salt
freshly ground pepper

Brussels sprouts with clementines *Serves 8*

Brussels sprouts boiled to death is my idea of hell, so I just sauté them with chilli to make this warm salad with clementines. You need some vegetables during the festive season to digest all that wonderful, but heavy, Christmas food!

Remove the outer leaves from the Brussels sprouts and cut off the bases. Cut them into very thin slices. Rinse and leave to drain in a colander.

Peel the clementines, cut them into slices and cut the slices in half. Melt the butter in a saucepan and sauté the sprouts for two minutes. Add the chilli and clementines and sauté for further two minutes. Remove from the heat, season and serve.

YOU WILL NEED
1kg Brussels sprouts
6 clementines
1 tsp salted butter
1 red chilli, finely chopped
salt
freshly ground black pepper

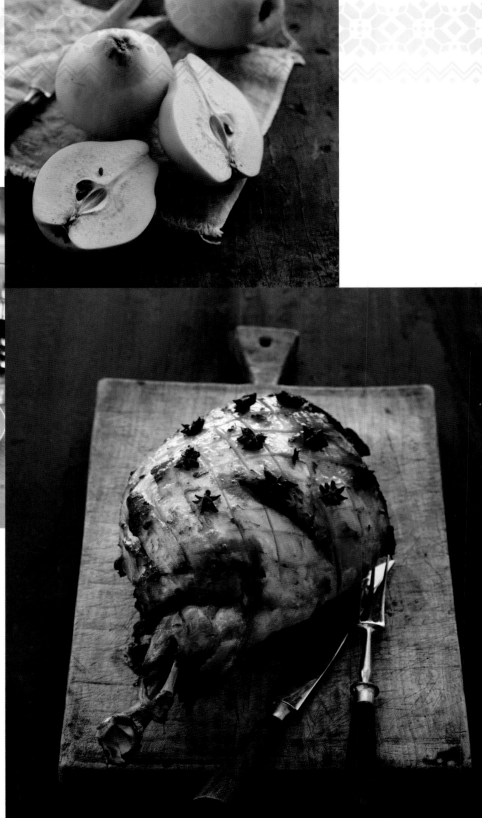

'When I was a child, we had to wash the dishes before we got our Christmas presents.'

THE CHRISTMAS EVE FEAST

Spiced quince ham *Serves 8*

Christmas ham with a mustard crust is traditional in Scandinavia, but I changed it to a quince version. This ham is not salted, so it's very tender and fresh tasting. Make sure you tell your butcher what the meat is for, and let him know it shouldn't be pre-cured.

Mix all the ingredients for the ham in a very large pot, adding enough water to cover. Bring to a boil, reduce the heat and simmer for 2–2½ hours, or until the temperature in the centre of the ham reads 55°C (130°) on a meat thermometer. Leave the ham in the liquid until it has cooled completely, then take it out and set aside for up to two days, covered and chilled, until you want to roast it.

On the day of serving, preheat the oven to 180°C/350°F/gas mark 4.

Remove the rind from the ham, leaving the fat behind, and cut a diamond pattern in the fat. Brush the quince syrup over the ham and press a star anise into 10 of the diamonds. Place in a roasting tray and roast for 20–25 minutes, until golden. Put it on the table and slice as you eat. Serve with Christmas Chutney (see page 36).

> **YOU WILL NEED**
> **For the ham**
> 3 star anise
> 2 red chillies, chopped
> 2 tbsp black peppercorns
> 1 head of garlic
> 2 onions, halved
> 300g root ginger, chopped
> 3 tbsp coarse sea salt
> 5kg piece leg of pork, bone in
>
> **For the glaze**
> 100–200ml Quince Syrup
>   (see below)
> 10 star anise

Quince syrup *Variable yield*

The amount you get varies, depending on how much juice there is.

Rinse the quinces, remove their stalks and blossom ends and chop roughly. Put in a saucepan with the lemon juice and enough water to cover, and bring to a boil. Reduce the heat, cover and simmer for about one hour, until very soft and tender. Pour the quinces into a jelly bag suspended over a bowl and leave to drain overnight. Don't press the bag or the syrup will be cloudy.

Next day, measure the juice, add the sugar and bring to a boil, stirring until the sugar dissolves. Let it boil, uncovered, over a medium heat until it becomes a thick syrup, stirring often. Carefully skim off any scum. Pour the syrup into a sterilised bottle and seal. Stored in a dark, cool place, this will keep for months.

> **YOU WILL NEED**
> 1kg quinces
> juice of 1 lemon
> 400g caster sugar per 1 litre
>   of quince juice

Rice pudding with hot cherry sauce *Serves 8*

For me, this is the best pudding in the world and I only eat it on Christmas Eve... then demolish the leftovers on the days after Christmas. Maybe that's the reason why I appreciate it so much. When we serve it on Christmas Eve, we also play a little game. One whole almond is added to the serving bowl, then we sit and eat in suspense: who gets the almond? Finding the almond means that you receive a present: the 'almond gift'. If you get the almond, you must hide it and not reveal yourself until everybody has eaten the whole bowl... that can be a daunting task.

YOU WILL NEED

For the rice pudding
2 vanilla pods
300g short-grain pudding rice
1.6 litres whole milk
2 tsp salt
2 tbsp caster sugar
150g blanched almonds
500ml double cream

For the cherry sauce
700g pitted cherries, fresh or frozen
150g caster sugar, or to taste
1 vanilla pod
3 tbsp cornflour

Cut one of the vanilla pods lengthways, without cutting it all the way through. Bring 300ml of water to a boil in a large, heavy-based saucepan, then add the rice and let it boil for two minutes, while stirring. Add the milk and split vanilla pod, stirring until it returns to a boil. Cover and cook for 25 minutes, stirring often so it doesn't burn. Remove from the heat and add the salt. Cover and set aside for 10 minutes, then stir in the sugar and leave until cold, or overnight.

Remove the vanilla pod and transfer the rice mixture to a large bowl.

Roughly chop all the almonds except for one, which must be left whole for the game! Cut the second vanilla pod lengthways, scrape out the seeds with the tip of a knife and add them to the rice. Whip the cream in a bowl until it forms soft peaks. Fold one-third of the cream into the rice to loosen, then fold in the rest. Add the chopped almonds. Taste the pudding: it should be sweet with a flavour of vanilla. Push the whole almond down into the pudding; it should be well hidden.

To make the sauce, mix the cherries, sugar and vanilla pod with 500ml of water in a saucepan. Bring to a boil, then reduce the heat and simmer for 15 minutes. Slake the cornflour in 3 tbsp of water in a cup or small bowl. Slowly add it to the cherries until they thicken, stirring constantly, and season to taste with more sugar, if you want. Serve the cold rice pudding with the hot cherry sauce.

**CHRISTMAS
LUNCH**

SPICED PORK 'BUTTER' AND RYE BREAD

BEETROOT PICKLED HERRINGS

ORANGE PICKLED HERRINGS

CHRISTMAS PICKLED HERRINGS

FRIED PLAICE WITH RÉMOULADE

MEATBALLS AND PICKLED BEETROOT

LIVER PATE WITH MUSHROOMS AND BACON

PORK WITH APPLES AND
JERUSALEM ARTICHOKES

HERBED ROLLED PORK

CHRISTMAS DAY SMÖRGÅSBORD

Just like the rest of the western world, Scandinavians go to a lot of Christmas lunches throughout December with friends, family and colleagues. Restaurants serve endless variations of the smörgåsbord, both traditional spreads and versions with a modern twist.

There is an order to a smörgåsbord: you start with cured herring, move on to hot fish, then to cold fish dishes, if there are any. After that, you get a clean plate and attack the hot meats on offer. You finish with sweets or cheese. Foreigners can have a hard time figuring out the rules!

Many families share a meal like this on Christmas Day, though in our family we have it on 26 December with beer and aquavit. (On Christmas Day, we stay at home with the children, eat leftovers in our pyjamas, play with new toys and read new books! In many ways this is my favourite day, especially when my children were little and we'd build a Lego town.)

❋ RYE BREAD ❋ SPICED PORK 'BUTTER' ❋ SALTED HERRINGS ❋ ORANGE PICKLED HERRINGS
❋ BEETROOT PICKLED HERRINGS ❋ CHRISTMAS PICKLED HERRINGS ❋ MARINATED FRIED HERRINGS
❋ FRIED PLAICE WITH RÉMOULADE ❋ LIVER PÂTÉ WITH MUSHROOMS AND BACON
❋ PORK WITH APPLES AND JERUSALEM ARTICHOKES ❋ HERBED ROLLED PORK ❋ MEATBALLS
❋ PICKLED BEETROOT ❋ DUCK, ORANGE AND ALMOND SALAD ❋ BLUE CHEESE AND PRESERVED PLUMS

'Prepare most
of the dishes in
advance, so you
have as little
work as possible
to do on the day.'

'We always go for a long walk before our Christmas smörgåsbord.'

Rye bread *Makes 1 large loaf*

The best loved and famous bread, for creating open sandwiches.

Mix the rye flour, buttermilk and salt. Cover with cling film and leave for two days. If it's too cold, it will go bad. Ideally, leave it in the kitchen at 21–25°C (70–75°F).

For the dough, in a large bowl, dissolve the sourdough in 750ml of lukewarm water. Add the salt, rye and plain flours and stir with a wooden spoon; it will be runny. Cover with a tea towel and leave for 12 hours at room temperature. I do this around dinner time and carry on the next morning. Add 250ml of lukewarm water, with the salt and cracked whole rye to finish, and stir. Take 100ml of dough, put it in a container and generously sprinkle with salt. Seal and refrigerate this sourdough for the next batch.

Pour the remaining dough into a three-litre loaf tin (oil it if it isn't non-stick). Cover with a tea towel for three to six hours, until it reaches the top of the tin. Preheat the oven to 175°C/350°F/gas mark 4. Bake for 1¾ hours, then cool on a wire rack.

YOU WILL NEED

For the sourdough culture
220g rye flour
300ml buttermilk
1 tsp coarse sea salt

For the dough
1 tbsp sea salt
375g rye flour
375g plain flour

To finish
2 tsp salt
500g cracked whole rye
oil, for the tin (optional)

Spiced pork 'butter'
Makes 2 x 200g jars

This is spread on rye bread, and herrings or cold cuts are served on top. My grandfather would eat it on its own, slathered on to a thick slice of rye bread and sprinkled with coarse salt.

Melt the fat in a heavy-based saucepan over a low heat, it takes quite a while. Pass the fat through a sieve into a clean saucepan, place over a low heat, and add the onions and cloves. Set any crackling aside. Let the fat simmer until the onions are golden brown, then remove from the heat and add one-third of the crackling. Season.

Pour the fat into sterilised jars and stir often while it is setting, to distribute the morsels of crackling evenly throughout.

Spread the spiced pork butter cold on slices of rye bread.

YOU WILL NEED
500g pork back fat, or flare, with
    some rind if possible
2 onions, finely chopped
10 cloves
salt
freshly ground black pepper

Three kinds of pickled herrings

I adore herrings, I eat them twice a week and have done all my life. There's a huge gulf between factory-cured and homemade fish. This salted herring recipe gives fillets that are much firmer than usual. If you prefer a softer texture, buy the salted fish for these recipes. (And for authenticity, use mild Scandinavian distilled vinegar instead of wine vinegar, from danishfooddirect.co.uk.)

Salted herrings

Rinse the herrings in cold water and remove any fins. Cut each fillet lengthways into two. Put one layer of herring into a sterilised, non-reactive container and cover with salt. Add another layer of fish and cover with salt again. Repeat until all the herrings are salted. Close with a lid, or cover with cling film, and leave in the fridge for one week. Now they are ready to be made into pickled herrings. (If you choose to cure a smaller amount of herring, simply scale down the amount of salt accordingly.)

> **YOU WILL NEED**
> 30 herring fillets
> about 1kg coarse sea salt

Orange pickled herrings
Serves 10–15

Put all the ingredients for the pickling solution into a large saucepan with 100ml of water and bring to a boil. Reduce the heat and simmer for 30 minutes, then cool.

Take the salted herrings from their container, rinse, then place in a big bowl and soak in cold water for at least four hours, changing the water three or four times. Drain, cut each into two pieces, place them in a non-reactive container and pour over the cold pickling solution. Mix in the orange zest.

Cover and store for three weeks in the fridge. To serve, cut the peel and white pith from the orange and cut it into thin slices, then slice the onion. Remove the herrings from the pickling solution and place them on a plate with the orange and onion.

> **YOU WILL NEED**
> **For the pickling solution**
> 1 shallot, sliced
> 500ml white wine vinegar
> 300g caster sugar
> 1 tbsp coriander seeds
> 1 tbsp black peppercorns
> 5 cloves
> 4 cardamom pods
>
> **For the fish**
> 20 salted herring fillets
> zest of 1 organic orange, pared in strips
> 1 large orange, to serve
> 1 onion, to serve

'Cured herring
has to be firm
and tasty.'

Beetroot pickled herrings

Serves 10–15

Peel and slice the beetroots, shallot and the horseradish.

Put all the ingredients for the pickling solution into a large saucepan with 100ml of water and bring to a boil. Reduce the heat and simmer for 30 minutes, then cool.

Take the salted herrings from their container, rinse, then place in a big bowl and soak in cold water for at least four hours, changing the water three or four times. Drain, cut each into two pieces, place them in a non-reactive container and pour over the cold pickling solution.

Cover and store for three weeks in the fridge. To serve, remove the herrings from the pickling solution, place them on a plate and mix with the onion.

YOU WILL NEED

For the pickling solution
200g beetroots
1 shallot
75g fresh horseradish
500ml cider vinegar
300g caster sugar
5 bay leaves

For the fish
20 salted herring fillets
1 onion, sliced, to serve

Christmas pickled herrings *Serves 10–15*

Put everything for the pickling solution into a large saucepan with 100ml of water and bring to a boil. Reduce the heat and simmer for 30 minutes, then cool.

Take the salted herrings from their container, rinse, then place in a big bowl and soak in cold water for at least four hours, changing the water three or four times. Drain, cut each into two pieces, place them in a non-reactive container and pour over the cold pickling solution.

Cover and store for three weeks in the fridge. To serve, remove the herrings from the pickling solution, put them on a plate and mix with the sliced onion.

YOU WILL NEED

For the pickling solution
500ml white wine vinegar
300g caster sugar
2 shallots, sliced
50g root ginger, sliced
1 tbsp coriander seeds
6 juniper berries
5 bay leaves
5 cloves
1 tbsp black peppercorns

For the fish
20 salted herring fillets
1 onion, sliced, to serve

Marinated fried herrings

Serves 8

These are my husband's favourite, and have a soft texture.

Put all the ingredients for the brine in a large saucepan and bring to a boil. Reduce the heat and simmer for 30 minutes, then cool. Rinse the herring and remove any fins. Mix the rye flour with salt and pepper on a large plate. Press each fillet, skin down, into the flour, so it sticks. Mash the goat's cheese with a fork, mix with the thyme and place 1 tsp on the flesh side of each fillet. Fold the ends in to cover, and press closed. Heat the butter in a frying pan and fry the fish for four to five minutes each side. Place in a large non-reactive dish. Cover with brine and leave for two hours.

Meanwhile, rinse and scrub the Jerusalem artichokes and cut into chunks. Heat the butter in a frying pan and sauté the artichokes until tender, but still with some bite. Season to taste. Cut the red onion into fine slices. Gently tip the Jerusalem artichokes into the dish with the herrings and sprinkle with the onion to serve.

YOU WILL NEED
For the brine
500ml white wine vinegar
300g caster sugar
2 bay leaves and 5 sprigs of thyme
1 tbsp peppercorns and 1 tsp salt

For the fish
12 fresh herring fillets
200g rye flour
200g goat's cheese
2 tbsp chopped thyme leaves
30g salted butter
1 large red onion, to serve

For the Jerusalem artichokes
700g Jerusalem artichokes
25g salted butter

Fried plaice with rémoulade *Serves 8*

Always in my Christmas lunch. Use another flat fish if you prefer.

Peel the celeriac and carrots, cut into very small cubes and blanch for two to three minutes in boiling salted water. Drain and leave to cool. Cut the apples into similarly sized cubes. Mix all the ingredients for the rémoulade and season to taste.

Rinse the plaice in cold water. Mix the rye flour on a plate with salt and pepper. Coat each fillet on both sides with the flour, patting off excess. Melt half the butter in a large frying pan and fry half the fish for two to three minutes on each side, without crowding the pan. Keep warm while you fry the remaining fish in the rest of the butter. Serve the fish warm with the rémoulade, lemon slices and parsley.

YOU WILL NEED
For the rémoulade
200g each celeriac and carrots
100g apples
300ml skyr, or Greek yogurt
2 tbsp mayonnaise
1 tsp turmeric
1 tsp caster sugar
2 tbsp each finely chopped
  tarragon, capers and gherkins
3 tbsp finely chopped red onion
finely grated zest from ½ lemon

For the fish
8 plaice fillets
200g rye flour
50g salted butter
lemon slices and parsley, to serve

Liver pâté with mushrooms and bacon *Serves 8*

This is my grandmother's recipe, and I have never really made another version. Most Scandinavian families have their own favourite way to make liver pâté, varying in which spices are used, whether you add anchovies or onions, and so on. I actually make this all year round, because it's part of the everyday Danish table, and most children eat it on rye bread with cucumber. However, it is always served lukewarm at Christmas lunch, with mushrooms and bacon.

YOU WILL NEED

5–6 small canned anchovy fillets

40g salted butter, plus more for the mould

40g plain flour

450ml semi-skimmed milk

1 large onion, grated

3 tsp salt

1½ tsp freshly ground black pepper

¼ tsp freshly grated nutmeg

1 tsp ground allspice

225g minced pork back fat, or flare

500g minced pig's liver

2 small eggs, lightly beaten

2–3 rashers of smoked bacon

3 bay leaves

To serve

150g rashers of smoked bacon

200g mushrooms, trimmed and thinly sliced

Mash the anchovies until they become a lumpy paste. Slowly melt the butter in a heavy-based saucepan, add the flour and mix to form a roux. Little by little, add the milk, constantly stirring. Bring to a boil and add the anchovies, onion, salt, pepper, nutmeg and allspice. Add the fat to the boiling sauce, stirring constantly until it melts. Add the liver and stir until it is evenly distributed. Remove the pan from the heat and cool slightly, then add the eggs and stir well. Preheat the oven to 175°C/350°F/gas mark 4.

Pour the pâté mixture into a buttered terrine mould, arranging the bacon rashers and bay leaves on top. Put the mould into a deep roasting tin. Pour hot water from the kettle into the roasting tin to come halfway up the sides of the mould. Carefully slide into the oven and bake, uncovered, for 1¼ hours.

Remove the pâté from the oven. To serve, fry the 150g of bacon in its own fat until crispy and golden, then remove from the pan. Fry the mushrooms in a little of the remaining bacon fat in the same pan.

Serve the pâté, lukewarm, in the mould, with the mushrooms and bacon on top.

'Classic Scandinavian liver pâté really does taste best on rye bread.'

'Serve the rolled pork on rye bread with Dijon mustard and thinly sliced onion.'

Pork with apples and Jerusalem artichokes *Serves 12*

Pork loin is a classic at Christmas; I added apples and Jerusalem artichokes. This can also be a main meal, with mashed potatoes.

Cut the tenderloins into steaks about 2cm thick. Rinse the Jerusalem artichokes, scrubbing well, and cut them into slices.

Heat the oil in a saucepan and fry the pork for three to four minutes on each side. Remove from the pan and keep warm. Add the artichokes and onions to the pan and sauté for five minutes. Add the apples and thyme, mix well and sauté for five minutes more. Add the vinegar, salt and pepper and cook for five minutes.

To serve, cut the largest pork steaks in half and place them all on a serving dish with the fruit and vegetables. Sprinkle with parsley to serve.

YOU WILL NEED
2 large pork tenderloins
300g Jerusalem artichokes
1 tbsp olive oil
2 onions, sliced
3 apples, cut into wedges
3 sprigs of thyme
3 tbsp cider vinegar
salt
freshly ground black pepper
chopped parsley, to serve

Herbed rolled pork *Serves 25*

A very traditional cold cut, my grandmother made 'rullepølse' every Christmas. This, Stig Jensen's recipe, is the best I know.

Place all the ingredients for the brine in a saucepan with 1 litre of water and bring to a boil until the sugar and salt have dissolved. Cool the brine down. Trim the meat, removing most of the fat. Sprinkle with the salt and spices. Soak the gelatine in cold water for five to 10 minutes, then squeeze out the excess and place the leaves on the meat to cover. Roll the meat very tightly lengthways, then tie it at 2.5cm intervals with kitchen string. Place in the brine for 48 hours in a cool place.

Put the 'rullepølse' in a saucepan, cover with fresh water and bring to a boil. Simmer for about one hour. It is done when it feels tender when pierced with a carving fork. Remove from the saucepan and place it in a loaf tin when still warm. Put another loaf tin on top and weight it down, to press. Chill for 24 hours, then slice thinly to serve.

YOU WILL NEED
For the brine
150g salt
75g caster sugar
2 bay leaves
1 small bunch of thyme
1 tbsp black peppercorns
5 cloves
1 onion, sliced

For the rullepølse
1 whole pork belly, without bones
50g coarse sea salt
20g freshly ground black pepper
5g ground allspice
6 gelatine leaves

Meatballs *Serves 8–10*

Meatballs are served in a variety of ways. They can be with or without sauce, with preserves, or with lingonberry jam. There's no doubt about it, this is a Scandinavian dish. In Danish they are called 'frikadeller'; in Swedish 'köttbullar'; in Norwegian 'kjøttkaker'; in Finnish 'lihapullat'.

Crush the juniper with the salt in a mortar. (If you don't have a mortar, then chop the juniper with a sharp knife. Remember the salt!) Mix the minced meats, juniper mixture, onion, sage, pepper and eggs together and beat well. Stir in the oats and breadcrumbs and beat again. Mix in the sparkling water and season generously once more with pepper.

Preheat the oven to 180°C/350°F/gas mark 4. Use a spoon and your free hand to shape the meat mixture into balls. Warm the butter in a large frying pan and fry the meatballs until crisp and golden on each side. Transfer the meatballs to an ovenproof dish and put them in the hot oven for 10 minutes to finish cooking. Serve with Pickled Beetroot (see below).

YOU WILL NEED
6 juniper berries
1 tsp coarse salt
300g minced pork
300g minced veal
1 onion, finely chopped
½ tbsp finely chopped sage
freshly ground black pepper
3 eggs, beaten
100g rolled oats
4 tbsp breadcrumbs
200ml sparkling water
salted butter, to fry

Pickled beetroot *Makes 1 litre jar*

Rinse the beetroots and simmer them in salted water for about 30 minutes, or until they are tender but still have some bite. Pour them into cold water to stop the cooking and, when cool enough to handle, rub off their skins.

Meanwhile, make the pickling solution. Put all the ingredients in a large saucepan, bring to a boil and stir until the sugar has dissolved. Leave until completely cold.

Cut the beetroots into 5mm slices, pack into sterilised jars, and pour over the pickling solution, including the spices and herbs. Seal. Leave to rest for one week before serving. These keep for months.

YOU WILL NEED
1kg beetroots
salt

For the pickling solution
50g root ginger, sliced
750ml cider vinegar
400g caster sugar
2 bay leaves
1 tbsp peppercorns

Duck, orange and almond salad *Serves 6–8*

There is often some roast duck meat left over at Christmas – in fact I always cook extra on purpose – and this tasty salad is a good way to use the last bits. The rich meat is perfect with the orange zest and a kick of acidity from the vinegar. If you don't have any leftover duck, you can cook a duck or chicken breast for this.

YOU WILL NEED

For the salad
200–300g leftover Roast Duck
    (see page 105)
150g baby spinach
2 celery sticks
75g almonds
finely grated zest of
    1 organic orange

For the dressing
4 tbsp Sea Buckthorn Vinegar
    (see page 40), or cider vinegar
1 tsp runny honey
3 tbsp grapeseed oil
salt
freshly ground black pepper

Preheat the oven to 180°C/350°F/gas mark 4. Cut or shred the duck into smallish bite-sized pieces. Rinse the spinach very well in several changes of water, to remove any grittiness, then drain it well. Peel the celery sticks with a vegetable peeler, to remove the strings, then slice very finely.

Put the almonds on a baking tray and place in the hot oven. Leave for five minutes, watching them carefully and shaking the tray, so they don't burn. When they are evenly roasted, remove them from the oven and chop them roughly.

Combine all the ingredients for the salad, tossing them together with your hands. Mix together all the dressing ingredients and season with salt and pepper. Toss the dressing through the salad just before serving.

Blue cheese and preserved plums *Serves 8*

The perfect end to a lovely meal. You simply have to drink port with it! Choose plums with sweetness and tender flesh.

YOU WILL NEED

For the preserved plums
500g plums
1 vanilla pod
200g caster sugar
50ml dark rum

To serve
250g Danish Blue, or any
   blue cheese
rye wafers

Rinse and halve the plums and remove their stones. Divide them between sterilised jars. Divide the vanilla pod lengthways and scrape out the seeds. Mix 500ml of water, the sugar, vanilla seeds and pod in a saucepan and bring to a boil. Reduce the heat and simmer, uncovered, for 10 minutes. Remove from the heat, then add the rum and pour over the plums. Each jar must be filled to the top. Seal the jars immediately.

The plums will be best after four or five days. (Stored in the fridge or a dark, cool place, they will keep for two or three months.) Before you serve them, bring them to room temperature.

Place the cheese on a platter with a jar of preserved plums and provide plenty of rye wafers. Serve with port.